Do What You Want

Also by Linda Lou

Bastard Husband: A Love Story

Do What You Want

How to Find a Job that Won't Crush Your Soul

Linda Lou

Career Strategist/Corporate Misfit

Aging Nymphs Media • Las Vegas, Nevada

DO WHAT YOU WANT
How to Find a Job that Won't Crush Your Soul

Copyright © 2022
Aging Nymphs Media

First Aging Nymphs Media edition published 2022
ISBN 978-0-9819796-1-8

All rights reserved.

Front and back cover photos by Lisa Wood Creative Photography

No part of this book may be used or reproduced in any manner whatsoever without written permission except in the case of brief quotations embodied in critical articles and reviews.

DO WHAT YOU WANT: How to Find a Job that Won't Crush Your Soul may be purchased at a bulk order discount for educational, business, or sales promotional use.

For information:
lindalou@agingnymphsmedia.com

For all my fellow oddballs

who just want to make a living

and enjoy life

Contents

1. Start Here 1

    A little about me 3

    I can help you if… 6

    Or this book may NOT be for you 7

    What you're in for 8

    Other stuff I want to say right now 12

2. Live with JOY 15

    Exercise: What brings you JOY? 16

    Integrate JOY into your daily life 20

    Exercise: Who's in your tribe? 25

3. Define Your Personal Brand 29

    Benefits of determining your personal brand 32

    Exercise: How to determine your personal brand 32

    Exercise: Write your personal branding statement 36

    Exuding your brand 38

    Exercise: Where do you hit a home run? 39

    Exercise: Write a personal mission statement 43

    Exercise: A few more questions 44

4. Plot Your Direction 47

    Exercise: Likes and Dislikes 47

    Exercise: Your preferred working conditions 51

5. Should I Stay or Should I Go? 61

Good reasons to stay in a job you can't wait to get out of 61

How to survive until you can leave 62

Good reasons to leave a job ASAP 66

Bad reasons to stay in a job that you really should leave 71

6. Your Financial Reality 75

Educate yourself about personal finance 75

Assess your current financial picture 76

Get out of debt ASAP 77

7. Explore the Possibilities 83

Exercise: Identify Preliminary Possibilities 84

Dig deeper and do a gap analysis 88

Are you willing to pay your dues? 90

Exercise: Identify Action Items 92

8. Assemble the Package 95

Write a kick-ass resume 95

Communicate your brand through social media 113

9. Rock Your Self-Confidence 117

Tips for projecting self-confidence 118

Overcoming "Yeah, but" fears 125

10. Get Yourself Out There 139
    Building and tapping into your network 139
    How to write a cover letter 148

11. Nail the Interview 157
    The initial call 159
    Screening interviews 160
    Working with third-party recruiters 161
    Addressing salary early on 162
    Interviewing – Before 164
    Interviewing – During 180
    Interviewing – After 187

12. Negotiate the Offer 191
    But I might be getting an offer from a sexier company 192
    Evaluate the position 193
    Evaluate the offer 196
    Prepare a win-win strategy 199
    Execute your strategy with confidence 202
    Start the new job right 203
    Uh-oh, that sexy company wants me now 207
    Uh-oh, this might have been a mistake 207

13. Live What You've Learned 209

1. START HERE

"ARE YOU STILL WORKING or are you retired?" I asked my new friend, Mary Ann, in a bustling lunch spot in New Orleans.

She frowned and shook her head. "I never really cared for work," she said with a slow Cajun twang. "I tried it one day, but I didn't enjoy it. I preferred to stay at home."

Blinking back tears, I leaned in and whispered, "You are my hero."

ಸಂಂ

I can't say that I've never enjoyed working. I love what I do, but navigating the workplace minefield is not for me and I'm not positive I've ever had a day at work that was better than a day at home. I've worn the corporate costume and played the career woman role like a B-movie actress for a good many years of my adult life, yet the reality is, a lot of those years weren't good at all. I was a corporate misfit, too happy and jokey for the workplace. Too spirited. Too honest. Too questioning. Too… me.

I don't think I'm alone on that. Too many of us hate going to work not because we hate to work, but because it crushes our souls to edit out so much of who we really are. You know that movie *Office Space?* It's a goddamn documentary. Yes, I'm generalizing, but there's a lot of boredom and bullshit and ass kissing that goes on in the world of work. A lot of feigned interest in "leveraging" and "incentivizing" and pretending the grand emperor spewing that crap isn't naked. A lot of suppressing a wince when you realize the dolt who so proudly proclaims he's a team player actually considers *you* to be a member of his team.

I was never good at playing the corporate game, even the ones I made up. One of my favorites was "If There Was a Gun to My Head and I Had to Have Sex with Somebody at this Conference Table, Whom Would I Choose?" Invariably, I'd conclude, "Pull the trigger. Please."

One time during a particularly soul-crushing "work sucks" period, I toyed with the idea of going into rehab. I didn't actually have a drug or alcohol problem (though I'm known to drink enough to make that totally believable); I just wanted a break from work and I'm a think-out-of-the-box kind of gal. I had it all figured out. At the time I had awesome health insurance that would cover almost the entire cost of a reputable 28-day program, plus I learned I'd also be able to collect short-term disability. The real draw, though, was all the interesting new friends I would make. I envisioned us having fun in a sterile rec room, painting crafty little art projects that would forever serve as souvenirs of our time together.

My real-life friends talked me out of that brilliant escape, but I did have a Plan B. For the previous year or so, I'd had a gigantic uterine fibroid that was causing super heavy periods. (Sorry for the TMI.) My gyno said, "Yeah, we can take it out or not. It's up to you." Well, hello! Once I found out I could score eight weeks of disability, you betcha I booked myself for a heaven-sent myomectomy on the first day of July. For two nights an angelic nursing staff waited on me in the hospital, and *shhhh...* a few days later I was as good as new with seven weeks left to "convalesce." After a glorious summer I returned to the cube farm rested and refreshed just in time for Labor Day weekend. Eight pounds lighter, I might add. Bonus.

Sure, there are people who claim they would still work even if they won the lottery, but most of us work because we like to have money. It's kind of an essential ingredient for a stable and happy life. And unless we were born into it, we're gonna have to do *something* to get that money.

Work doesn't have to suck, though. It *shouldn't* suck! Making a living takes up a huge chunk of your waking hours, and I've come to realize it's possible to play the game without selling your soul or waking up on a Sunday morning with that "Shit, I have to work tomorrow" feeling of deflation. I've had jobs that I really loved, with fun as hell coworkers who became lifelong friends, with bosses I truly admired, in organizations that weren't toxic and that provided me with the opportunity to share my talents in a way that could have a lasting impact on people's lives. Sure, I've taken a lot of missteps, too, but I know it's possible to find work you actually won't dread. The key is to know what you're super good at and to do it in a place where people appreciate both your work and who you are as a person.

A little about me

Over the course of the past three decades, I've worked mostly in the field of corporate outplacement, and those were by far the years I found most rewarding. In case you don't know what corporate outplacement is (also referred to as "career transition"), let me explain. There are a lot of euphemisms in that business, so I'll be direct. When a company lets people go—maybe there's a mass layoff or maybe only one person is tapped on the shoulder—they will often offer their departing employees personalized help with their job search provided by an outside consulting firm. Over the years, I've worked for three of these firms. There is never a cost to the affected person; these services are paid for by their former employer and are offered as part of the individual's severance package.

In the first outplacement firm I worked for, I mostly helped clients with the written aspects of their job search, primarily their resumes and cover letters. I was surprised to find that many senior level executives had a hard time writing anything. Writing always came naturally to me. I figured it was something everyone could do. As an undergrad I never took an English class; I passed a basic proficiency exam at the beginning of my freshman year and was psyched to get three credits for free. It didn't occur to me that writing was a natural talent I should maybe look into. Anyway, after working with those execs who couldn't put two words together, I wanted to learn more, so I went back to school in my thirties for a master's degree in technical communication. That was the beginning of my work in career development and in writing.

I find a real sense of satisfaction in creating a kick-ass resume for someone whose self-esteem may be fragile from being let go; it's like putting together a beautiful puzzle. I enjoy facilitating networking roundtables and presenting all kinds of workshops related to the job search. Since telling people what to do is one of my superpowers, I love helping my clients figure out what they do best and what their next step might be, and they seem to truly appreciate my humor and down-to-earth approach as much as my expertise.

I figure I've helped thousands of people, ranging from hourly employees to senior executives, find their place in the world of work. Gotta love the irony—I've spent most of my career helping people find the one thing I've never really wanted: a job. Just as my father the bus driver used to say, "I don't work, I take other people to work," I like to say, "I don't work, I help other people find work." Oh, and since 2003, I've had a side hustle as a comedian, which makes me even more of an oddball. Corporate career consulting and stand-up comedy... interesting combination, right? Reminds me of a store in my hometown—Albany, New York—that sold pianos and waterbeds.

If you've read my first book, *Bastard Husband: A Love Story*, you know I got into comedy during what I call my "dark days." If you haven't yet read it, of course I highly recommend that you do, although I'll warn you, I swear a lot in it. I wasn't in a particularly good mood when I wrote it. Anyway, that book is a memoir that chronicles my first year alone in Las Vegas after my second divorce (yay, me...) and how I shook the Etch-a-Sketch of life and started over.

Those early years in Sin City sucked, with the pain of another broken marriage compounded by the pain of having to find a job. Las Vegas may seem like a good-sized city, but it's really a small town where, as they say, it's not what you know, it's who you know. And I knew no one. Those dark days were marked with several false starts, contract gigs, and a technical writing job I abhorred. If you've ever toyed with filling half your coffee thermos with Bailey's Irish Crème, you know what I mean.

I was able to do a tiny bit of consulting with a local outplacement firm, but the work they threw my way was sporadic and not enough to sustain me. Almost a decade later, the managing partner of the firm called to say he was looking for someone to work with clients and manage the operations of the Las Vegas office. Would I be interested? Um, *yes*! I spent six mostly wonderful years in that position and then decided to do my own thing, which was to write resumes and offer career counseling as a freelancer.

Today life is good. I have time to devote to comedy, writing, and dancing. For the past twelve years I've been with a handsome and funny guy who is definitely on the crazy side (he's a great source of comedy material), and who fulfills what a friend of mine says are the two most important requirements of a loving relationship: 1) He "gets" me, and 2) He worships the ground I walk on. Mike is incredibly supportive of all my endeavors and even brags about my cooking, which is curious since I've never owned a spice other than cinnamon.

My kids are doing well, and although they're in their forties (I was super young when they were born), they're still freakin' adorable. My grandchildren are an endless source of joy, my siblings are all good, and on top of all that, my 87-year-old mother is healthy and vibrant and spunky as hell. She's grateful for every good day and has taken to having dessert after breakfast because, hey, you never know. She's right.

Looking back, I realize I had to go through those tough early days in Las Vegas in order to get to where I am today. Nobody gets out of this world without enduring some miserable periods. Somehow we live through them, though we pay a price. It took me years to heal emotionally, and a decade to recover from the stupidity of spending money when I wasn't making any. I reasoned that for all I'd been through, I "deserved" to continue the lifestyle I was used to (not that anyone would describe it as lavish). But trying to sustain it without a source of income and by living on credit cards was downright foolish. One must always do the math. That was an important lesson to learn, and one that I'll never forget.

Like everyone else I'm a work in progress, and I'm the first to admit I'm as nutty as the next person. Probably nuttier. I have a wicked bird phobia. I can't eat if a cabinet door is open. I've lost sleep wondering if your ears really do keep growing throughout your life and if so, what will I look like when I'm a hundred and four?

I'm not entirely sure I should be giving anybody advice, but I honestly feel I have created a life for myself that's far beyond anything I could have imagined. I'd love to share what I've learned along the way, specifically how work—what you do to make money—ties into your overall happiness and satisfaction.

I can help you if...

If you can relate to any of these scenarios, you're the person I had in mind while I wrote this book.

- You're content enough in your job, or maybe the better word is "resigned." You plug along, tied to the golden handcuffs because of the better-than-average benefits and the weeks of vacation time you've accrued. After work you go home, make dinner, watch some TV, make tomorrow's lunch, get your work clothes ready, and call it a night. The next day you go through the same routine. Maybe you stay because the work isn't too taxing and you can get through the day on autopilot. You don't dare look for something more rewarding since things could be worse somewhere else—the grass is always greener—and this job is a known evil.

- You're in a job that's not what you expected, and you know in your heart that you're barking up the wrong tree. Everyone said a degree in computer science (or whatever) has the best job prospects, but now that you're working in that field… ugh. You wonder if you've made a terrible mistake.

- You're "really" an artist or musician or comedian and need a day job to pay your bills until you can start making a living from your creative work. Work-life balance is essential to allow for the time and energy you need to pursue your artistic goals.

- You suspect your current position could be in jeopardy. Rumors are flying, you haven't been included in projects lately, and you sense the end is near. You want to update your resume and start thinking about your next move, but you have no idea what that actually might be.

- You're at or near retirement age and want to create a satisfying Act III for your life, where it all comes together. You've been there, done that when it comes to advancing your career; you'd be happy just coasting. At this point, you want to work on *your* terms doing something meaningful and intrinsically rewarding, something stress-free that will keep your mind sharp, maybe something you could do part-time or even on a volunteer basis.

- You're ready to enter the workforce for the first time in ages. Maybe you've been raising a family or caring for an elderly relative. The problem is, you're not sure what you can do or where you can do it. You have no idea how to go about searching for a job, and truth be told, the thought of it terrifies you.

- You still don't know what you want to be when you grow up. You've always envied people who envisioned their career path since they were in first grade. Usually they wanted to be something like a teacher or a fireman or a nurse, and that's exactly what they grew up to be and they loved their job and retired with a great pension and lived happily ever after. So annoying. Don't feel bad if you don't yet have this nailed; you're not alone. The comedian Paula Poundstone has a brilliant take on this; she says adults ask kids what they want to be when they grow up because we're looking for ideas.

- You hate your job and everything about that stinkin' place and want out NOW!!!

Or this book may NOT be for you

I've worked with quite a few clients that I was unable to help because they already knew everything. Whenever I heard, "I already know how to conduct a job search" or "My resume is already done and it's excellent," I could guarantee that not only would their resume be a total piece of crap, but their personality would be equally appealing. The good news is, you're not one of those people because there's no way they'd be reading this book.

If you're delicate and bruise easily, this book is definitely not for you. While I fancy myself as a fun and lovely person, my communication style lies somewhere between Judge Judy and Susie Essman's character on *Curb Your Enthusiasm*.

Also, I'm not the most politically correct person, and the older I get, the less I'm inclined to choose every freakin' word with care in order to express myself in a way that no one can possibly find offensive. Don't get me wrong, I would never intentionally hurt anybody's feelings. Even if you're wearing something hideous, I would probably say, "That's not really my style" and leave it at that. I believe being offended is a choice and people in general need to toughen up. If someone clearly is not intending to be hurtful—and anyone with halfway decent social skills should be able to determine that— then don't get all bent out of shape. There's no honor in pouncing on a person for an unintentional misstep in their communication. This is one of the reasons why performing comedy is getting to be less joyful for me; everyone's so goddamn sensitive.

As with *Bastard Husband: A Love Story*, I wrote this for "my people." If you're with me so far, you're probably one of them. Nobody is everybody's cup of tea, though, so if you don't like me or what I have to say, that's cool. Close this book and give it to Goodwill or pass it on to someone you're not particularly fond of.

What you're in for

What I want to share here is a collection of insights, practices, and life lessons that I hope will inspire and motivate you to create a work life that provides financial stability, brings you intrinsic satisfaction, and allows you to have a personal life that is filled with joy. In other words, this book could have been titled *Shit I've Learned that Other People Might Find Helpful*.

I'll try not to sound preachy as I deliver these gems of wisdom or use what my daughter calls my "bossy voice." I'll also try not to sound like an eternally optimistic, and equally unrealistic, motivational speaker. I'm self-aware enough to know my *joie de vivre* can be both charming and annoying as hell. I can't help it; I'm a huge lover of life. The Irish have a cool word, *craic*, which has no direct translation in English but essentially means "the art of enjoyment." Usually heard in the context of music and drinking, it's about having fun, grooving on the company of others, and being able to laugh at almost any situation. I'm all about the *craic*.

This is how it's gonna go down.

Know who you are and what you want

In order to have a happy and rewarding life, both at home and at work, you need to have a clear idea of what that life looks like for you. This is often the hardest part. Once you know what you want, you can make a plan and then take the steps to go out and get it. But if you don't know what you want, you'll be stuck with whatever the world gives you. Think of it this way: You would never go up to the deli guy in the supermarket and say, "I'd like some meat," right? You'd say, "I'd like a half pound of ham, a quarter pound of roast beef…" and so on. Of course, if you're a vegan I imagine you wouldn't go near the deli at all other than to announce that you're a vegan. (I joke, dear vegans.) My point is, if you're not specific about what you want, you'll end up with whatever the deli guy decides to give you. Which will probably be nothing because nobody wants the responsibility for making your choices.

This is why people tend to drift into a job and then drift into the next. They take what the world sends them versus proactively figuring out who they are and what they want, and then devising and executing a plan to get it. You've probably heard people say that when you're looking for a job, you're out there selling yourself. *Most people don't know what the product is!* They haven't taken the time to do the work that you're going to do, and by doing this work, you'll have a tremendous advantage over your competition. You're also much more likely to land in a place that's a good match for your talents, values, and preferences.

So the next few chapters of this book focus on self-awareness and discovery. I'll be giving you a bunch of exercises to help you look within and explore the many different facets of what makes you… you.

You'll be articulating some good things about yourself, such as your skills and what you do better than almost anyone on earth, and you're going to put these in writing. We've been conditioned since childhood not to brag about ourselves, so this may feel uncomfortable. I get that, but you're not writing fiction. Own it. I'm also going to ask you to think big. Your brain may resist going there because we're conditioned to think within limits and within the realm of what we believe is possible. You can get past that.

You'll identify what brings you joy, where your interests lie, your values and what you stand for, and your life's mission. We'll look at your current work situation and where you've worked in the past. You'll notice patterns of workplace characteristics that you've liked and some that you never want to experience again. You'll identify what you want to change.

As you're going through this book, don't just glance through these exercises and think, "Oh, that looks like a good idea" and then move on. No, actually *do* them! Take the pen-to-paper approach. Get a notebook to do the exercises and record your thoughts or write in this book—whatever is easiest for you. You may want to go through this book with friends who are also interested in making a career move and bounce ideas off each other. That will give you some accountability.

It's not unusual for people to struggle with these exercises. That's because our attention almost always is directed outward, not inward. Our thoughts are consumed by our kids, partners, parents, and friends. We rarely take the time to focus on ourselves. Allow yourself to be selfish for once (being selfish is not necessarily a bad thing) and to be the center of your own damn universe.

Have fun with these exercises. Approach them with a playful spirit. Don't feel as if you have to complete any of them in one sitting. Not everything will come to you at once. Ideas pop up when you least expect them. Capture insights as they hit you. Return to this book or your notebook often, at least once a day.

Consider your options, identify what's feasible, and create a plan

After you've collected all this information about yourself, you'll have some options to consider. I'll give you some good, and bad, reasons to either stay in a job or leave it, as well as some coping mechanisms to help you survive a job you hate until you can get the hell out. You'll determine the type of work structure that best meets your current needs whether it's full-time, part-time, temporary or contract work, volunteer work, or self-employment. You'll set some short- and long-term goals, and then you'll create an action plan to achieve them.

Before you move forward, you'll have to make sure your plan is financially feasible. Your personal financial picture determines what options make sense right now. As I know from my own experience, the math always has to work out. We'll talk about the importance of having an emergency fund and how getting and staying out of debt can change your life forever.

Overcome fear and project confidence

The biggest obstacle that could get in the way of your success is self-imposed: fear. Maybe it's fear of rejection, fear of making a wrong turn, fear of failure, fear of success, or fear of losing a sense of security (as if there is such a thing). I'll address these fears as well as other crazy shit we tell ourselves, like we're too old, too fat, too far down the path we've been on to make a change, or we don't have the right background or enough education.

I'll also talk about the benefits of venturing out of your comfort zone, and I'll give you some concrete steps you can take to project confidence.

Get yourself out there

You'll soon be eager to get out there and share your wonderful talents and your wonderful self with the world. I'll go over networking, a word that makes a lot of us roll our eyes back to our brain stem because we think of it as being forced and phony. I'm with you. To me there's nothing more nauseating than the prospect of having to "work a room," and I consider myself to be outgoing—I can't imagine how introverts must feel. I'll show you how to build your network of contacts and how to reach out to people who can help you in a way that is comfortable and authentic.

We'll also talk about communicating your personal brand through social media. I understand if you want to stay out of cyberspace and detest social media. Humor me and read this section anyway.

Master the nuts and bolts of the job search

This section is the "how to" part of getting yourself out there. Trust me when I say I'll try to make it as painless as possible. I'm going to give you my step-by-step approach to

- Writing a kick-ass resume that isn't just a bunch of regurgitated job descriptions
- Creating a LinkedIn profile that makes you sound like a person, not a product
- Writing a targeted cover letter that communicates why you're a great fit for that opportunity
- Rocking the interview — what to do before, during, and after

- Negotiating an offer with confidence because, hey, you're asking only for what you deserve

Live what you've learned

By the time you get to this part of the book, you'll have done so much great work. We'll wrap things up by reinforcing the importance of truth, joy, authenticity, humor, financial stability, and other essential ingredients that make a happy life.

Other stuff I want to say right now

Almost every topic I touch on is vast enough to warrant a book in itself, so I urge you to seek out resources and dig deeper into the areas where you need more help. You'll notice I rarely point you to specific websites or other resources. That's because things change with time, and I'd like to keep the updates to this book at a minimum. As you can tell, I'm giving you my spin on things based on my experience and life lessons. If my advice doesn't sit right with you, trust your gut and don't do it.

Writing a book is super hard. No, I should say writing a *good* book is super hard. There's a lot of crap out there, a lot of blah-blah-blah streams of consciousness that people package up in about twenty minutes so they can call themselves an author. I can't do that. I take pride in my product, and in order to live with myself, I have to offer something of high quality that you can actually benefit from. If you're taking the time to read this, I owe it to you to give you my best, and I apologize right now for occasionally using corny words like "authenticity" and "intention" and "mindfulness." Sometimes there's really no better word out there, which is why 70-year-old men are still called "boyfriends." But if I ever, *ever* say "journey," please throw this book into a blazing inferno.

What's my motivation? Well, how you spend your time making a living has a huge effect on your overall happiness. I don't want you to hate what you do. I want you to have an amazing life that's full of joy. When you're happy, you're fully there for those you love. You're a stronger role model for the people you influence. You're kinder to service workers and old folks. Why do I care? You might run into my mother in the supermarket. I want you to be nice to her. I don't want you to be an asshole because you had a bad day at work.

The world can turn into a shit show at any given moment, but there's still beauty and goodness all around us. Though you may seem powerless in trying to change anything on a grand scale, you can start by making your own little world—including your world at work—as beautiful and loving as possible.

Now let's get going and have some fun.

2. LIVE WITH JOY

I WANT TO BEGIN by talking about joy. Why? Because joy is an essential ingredient of life, right up there with food and shelter. Joy makes us happy; it nourishes the soul. Having joy in our lives gives us the will and the strength to persevere through challenges. In addition to making money to pay for food, shelter and other essentials, we work so we can experience JOY.

In my workshops, I ask participants to make a list of everything that brings them joy. The first few items come easily; after that, they struggle. People aren't used to thinking that way, which is no surprise since these days everyone seems overscheduled and out of balance.

When you take the time to identify what brings you joy, you learn what makes you happy, what's significant to you, where your passions lie. You can then set your priorities accordingly to ensure that the path you decide to pursue leads to where you actually want to go.

For example, let's say coaching your kid's soccer team brings you joy; it's one of the most meaningful things you do. I've worked with men and women who've missed huge chunks of time with their children due to business travel and/or late hours in the office. Maybe that didn't matter to them, but if being there for your kid's games matters to you, work-life balance is something you'll want to explore during an interview before you accept a new position.

Here's another example: I've lived out West for nearly twenty years. Almost my entire family is in upstate New York, and my rule has always been that if I can't get to Albany every three or four months, then I'd have to move back there. My kids are grown adults, but I can't bear to be away from them for too long. I value every second I spend with my grandchildren. I can sit with my mother on her couch doing absolutely nothing and be overcome with happiness just by her presence. So there's no way I would accept a job that doesn't provide liberal vacation time. I would also need to make enough money to afford the airfare.

We begin here because you want the joy factor to drive the decisions that will impact your life moving forward. ***Think of joy as the foundation from which the rest of your life is built.*** If you want to find work that brings you joy, you have to know what joy looks like and what it means to you.

Exercise: What brings you JOY?

In this exercise, you're going to list twenty things that bring you joy. These may be activities you regularly like to do, wish you had more time to do, or something you've done only once and would like to do again. Be as specific as possible, as shown in the examples below.

Vague: Spending time with my family
Specific: Watching funny movies with the kids
Specific: Camping in the woods with my siblings and cousins
Specific: Playing penny-ante poker with Mom and Dad

Vague: Traveling
Specific: Spending a week in Sedona
Specific: Taking a road trip through Vermont
Specific: Backpacking through Germany

Vague: Music
Specific: Going to the Wednesday night live music series in the park
Specific: Playing my guitar after dinner
Specific: Blasting "Gimme Shelter" while driving through the desert

Also consider what you like to be around, or possessions or guilty pleasures that make you happy. Don't worry if they seem stupid or insignificant; they're neither. Again, capture the details.

Example: Fresh flowers on the dining room table
Example: Correctly answering the Final Jeopardy question when none of the contestants could
Example: A *People* magazine with the royal family on the cover

It's okay if you can't think of twenty things in one sitting, come back and add to this list whenever you want.

DO WANT YOU WANT

20 Things that Bring Me Joy

Take a look at what you've come up with. You may see a couple of big-ticket items such as a cruise or a beach vacation, but I bet the majority of what you have requires zero to little financial commitment. Most people's lists are loaded with activities such as "reading a good science fiction novel," "watching my dog play with his friends at the dog park," or "binge-watching true crime dramas on Netflix." (Note how those examples are more explicit than "reading a good book," "playing with my dog," or "binge-watching shows on Netflix.")

Now indicate next to each item the last time you actually did it. Chances are it's been way too long, so here are a couple of questions:

- Why aren't you doing joyful things more often?

- What are the biggest time wasters that take you away from what brings you joy?

- What can you do today that will bring you joy? What can you schedule on your calendar? List at least three things and commit to making them happen.

Integrate JOY into your daily life

Here are some tips that will help make joy the centerpiece of your everyday life:

Eat only what brings you JOY

When I order a hamburger in a restaurant, I ask the wait staff to hold the bun. There's nothing about a boring hamburger bun that brings me joy. Instead, I will enjoy those twenty-seven grams of carbs in the form of a nice cold Guinness or a scoop of mocha almond fudge ice cream. Because I eat with intention, as opposed to automatically consuming whatever is in front of me, I don't feel guilty about enjoying the things I love. Beer and ice cream or a hamburger bun? The joy factor is nowhere near equal. Unfortunately, beer and ice cream are also two major contributors to the middle-aged spread that now dictates my entire wardrobe. However, giving them up would pose a quality-of-life issue I'm not prepared to face.

Don't go crazy; you have to be practical. Starring in a reality show for the morbidly obese is not the best goal, so every once in a while throw some broccoli on your plate. That's the only nutritional advice you'll get from me, and for good reason. I refuse to eat a banana and I'll extract celery from my macaroni salad with the precision of a neurosurgeon, but hotdogs bring me joy despite the rumors that they're ground pig anuses.

Wear only what brings you JOY

When I'm in the dressing room at Ross Dress-for-Less (or Marshall's if I'm shopping for a special occasion), four questions determine whether or not I walk out of the store with something new: 1) Does this fit? 2) Do I need it? 3) Does this bring me joy? and 4) Do I want to spend the money to buy this now? The answers to all of these questions must always be "yes." Let's address each one.

Does it fit? Never buy clothes that don't fit, and I mean fit today at this very moment. I'm not sure if men go through this, but every woman has purchased the *cutest* outfit that we know will look perfect after we lose just a couple of pounds. "This will give me incentive to lose weight," we tell ourselves. Except rarely, if ever, do we actually achieve the weight loss required to wear that cutest little outfit. Seasons change and it hangs in the closet with tags on the sleeves, mocking you for forgetting to hold the hamburger bun and having the Guinness and ice cream anyway. Then a few more seasons come and go, and when you can no longer look at that stupid thing that isn't even *that* cute anyway, you altruistically deliver it to the women's shelter as you try to convince yourself that somebody will surely appreciate this once trendy garment that's now out of style.

Sometimes super cute clothes simply don't fit, and that can be heartbreaking. But if the shoulders are weird or if it's a wee bit short-waisted, that crinkled chiffon dress cannot go home with you. Carry it around the store for as long as you want and then before you leave, release back to its place on the rack with love.

Do I need it? Never buy anything you don't need. I own more black clothing than a 1960s Italian widow; it's beyond my comprehension that perhaps people might like to see me in an actual color. As a result, every time I feel drawn to yet another black sweater or dress, I have to hold a difficult conversation with myself. You, too, can live without another pair of jeans that's imperceptibly different from the fourteen other pairs you already own. Be strong and say no.

Does this bring me joy? Promise yourself right this moment that you won't buy anything that doesn't bring you joy. Clothes that don't fit properly will not bring you joy. If you already have ten soft gray t-shirts, one more will not bring you joy. You're no longer a consumer, you're a collector.

I have three little nightgowns that bring me joy. I don't need any more. Sometimes I'll see a cute one in the store, but since I already have three that I really love, it's easy for me to keep walking. If something happens to one of my nightgowns, I'll find another one. Until then, I'm good. Have you ever read about an old lady who wore the same nightgown for thirty years and when she died her family was shocked that she'd been sitting on a fat bank account? That could be me.

Loving your clothes can be a challenge if your work situation requires a wardrobe you'd never wear in real life. Back in the 80s and 90s I had to wear business attire to work every day. It broke my heart to buy suits and shoes that I knew I would never have fun in. That said, I gladly incurred the cost of hiking up the hemline on my skirts as high as I could get away with. Suits are not me, but miniskirts most certainly are.

Sometimes we buy clothes only because we feel we need something new to wear to work. When you shop with this kind of mindset, "something" translates to "anything." That's when you end up buying stuff that doesn't bring you joy, and what doesn't bring you joy will hang in your closet with the other ugly work clothes you've worn only a couple of times because you never really liked them.

Train your mind to say yes to work clothes only if they bring you joy, especially if you're unhappy at work. If you hate your job, you can't hate what you're wearing, too. That's too much sadness. Never buy anything that isn't "you," and don't worry if you're wearing the same things over and over. No one notices, no one cares, and if you hate your job that much, you don't care what anybody thinks anyway. The bottom line is, you can sit in your cubicle looking depressed or you can sit there looking adorable. The choice is yours.

When you love your clothes and feel you look good in them, you carry yourself differently. You project more confidence. You're gonna have a better day. When you buy only clothes that bring you joy, your entire closet will bring you joy. When you're choosing what to wear, everything you see will be something you feel good about; you won't have to sift through a lot of crap that should never have come into the house in the first place. Your closet and dresser become more manageable. Changing clothes out for the seasons won't be such a chore. And you won't be spending money needlessly. That means you'll have more to spend on JOY.

Do I want to spend money on this now? This sounds much more pleasant than "Can I afford this?" but that's really what I'm getting at. Don't hate me, but unless you can pay cash for an item, the answer to this question is "no." If you're carrying any type of balance on a credit card, it's best to restrict your spending to essentials such as food and gas. We'll talk more about this later. The good news is, if you buy only what brings you joy, pay cash for it and pass on everything else, in time you'll have the money to buy whatever you want. Believe it.

Release what doesn't bring you JOY

This is important. Your stuff weighs you down, and I truly believe that clutter in your physical space also clutters your mind. Sell or give away possessions that no longer serve you or bring you joy so someone else can appreciate them. Ease the burden imposed by the hell of ownership.

I know it's hard to get rid of something you received as a gift. You have no use for it, but you can't throw it away because it came from someone special. When my son was in high school I took him to New York City a few times to see one of his favorite bands, Sonic Youth. We'd get a hotel so we could spend time exploring Manhattan, and these memories still bring me such joy. I was so touched when one Christmas he gave me a book about Greenwich Village as a memento of our trips together.

The book was hard to get into, more like a textbook than something you'd read for enjoyment. For years I'd look at it, knowing it was not bringing me joy, but when I'd periodically weed out the duds on my bookshelves, I'd hang on to that one. I felt bad that I didn't like the book, but I couldn't bring myself to part with it; my sweet Christopher had given it to me. I came to realize that just because somebody gives you something, they don't expect you to hold onto it forever, and they certainly wouldn't want their gift to become a source of guilt. One Saturday morning I finally handed the book over to the guy in the Goodwill truck.

It's even harder to let go of a present given to you by someone who has passed on. Take a photo of it and you can look at it anytime. Tell yourself their spirit will be more at rest knowing that their gift from how many years ago, that they probably don't even remember giving you, is no longer bringing you down.

Some of us have trouble tossing things that are still functional. Why would you throw out a perfectly good three-hole paper puncher that you haven't used in the seven years since you bought it at a lawn sale for fifty cents? Unless it brings you joy, that question should answer itself.

Don't do things that don't bring you JOY

Every time you agree to do something you really don't want to do, you erode a little bit of your self-esteem. You still have to go to the dentist and get your oil changed, but you don't have to go to a Pampered Chef party at a coworker's house on a precious Sunday afternoon. Don't want to attend a gender reveal party for someone you barely know? Not comfortable driving into an unsafe neighborhood for a house party? Can't incur the cost of attending a good friend's destination wedding? It's okay to politely decline. All you have to say is, "Sorry, I can't make it. I hope you guys have fun," and leave it at that.

People who press you for reasons why you can't go or who try to impose guilt on you are stepping over the line. You don't owe anybody any further explanation. Nobody has to know you're not available because you've set aside some time for yourself. What's not okay is to accept an invitation and back out at the last minute or pull a no-show. That's rude and not cool.

Say no when it's the wisest thing to say and remember that sometimes we're bound by family obligations that we just have to honor. And if at all possible, *always* make the effort to attend a wake, funeral, or memorial service. Your presence will mean more than you know.

Surround yourself with people who bring you JOY

If you're lucky, you have some people in your life who support you to no end—they're almost like fans. They think everything you do is amazing. You could rob a bank and they'd say, "Aw, that's okay. You must have needed the money." You know they're not just blowing smoke; these are your A-listers, your BFFs, the people who are there for you anytime no matter what. They motivate and inspire you. They make you laugh. They make you feel better about yourself and the world at large. And no doubt you do the same for them. These are the members of your tribe.

Cherish these individuals. They are the ones you turn to when you're feeling low and who celebrate your victories without an iota of envy. When I look at the names of the people in my tribe, I feel grateful and lucky. I consider it an honor to be part of their tribe as well.

CHAPTER 2. LIVE WITH JOY

Exercise: Who's in your tribe?

Write the names of the people in your tribe below.

The People in My Tribe

Do Want You Want

Protect yourself from people who don't bring you JOY

On the other hand, there are those who can drain the life out of you. Some of them are good souls who truly mean well; others, not so much. We won't name them specifically, but do any of these characters look familiar?

The bummer. We all know at least one Gloomy Gus or Debbie Downer. To them, life is terrible and the outlook for the future is bleak—whether it's their future, your future, or the future of the entire universe. There's no such thing as good news for these killjoys. If you won the lottery and gave them half the money, they'd remind you of the taxes you'd have to pay. These glum chums seem to have an affinity for tragedy and a talent for recounting stories of misfortune with a somber delivery worthy of a Sarah McLachlan soundtrack.

The "Yeah, but..." When friends or family members tell us about their problems, our natural inclination is to try to help. That's nearly impossible with this type because invariably whatever insights or advice you offer is met with "Yeah, but..." followed by why your line of thinking won't work for their particular situation. They would rather recite the same wretched "woe is me" monologue over and over than address the issue that seems to dominate every conversation.

The "Me, Me" Mimi. These people have a way of always making the conversation about themselves. Whatever you have to share is sure to be met with a more dramatic story from the archives of their own lives. Usually that story is not remotely related to the topic at hand, but they're itching to tell it and they have an audience: you. They never ask you a question—no surprise—because the truth is, they don't care to hear your answer.

The control freak. A few years ago, I was in a movie theater scrolling through my phone as I waited for the show to begin. I should add the unflattering detail that this was a free screening as part of an AARP film series. Anyway, the nanosecond the lights go down, the woman next to me looks in my direction and says, "Cell phones off!" with a tone of authority one might use to address a classroom of unruly fifth graders. I sat there positively seething through the entire movie, consumed with hatred for that frumpy bitch, mainly because I myself have zero tolerance for impolite theater behavior and how dare she think *I* would be the type to be fiddling with my cell phone?

Chapter 2. Live with Joy

Control freaks feel it's their birthright to tell you what to do, how to act, who to hang with, what's good for you, what's bad for you… they'd love nothing more than to take charge of every detail of your life. "You *have* to try this!" they'll command, and follow up with, "Did you try that? I told you to try that." They relish nothing more than orchestrating how others should live, though ironically their own lives are often quite a mess.

The non-stop talker. You know who I'm talking about. Simply put, these yakkers need to STFU. They continuously spew out crap in one giant run-on sentence without ever coming up for air. If by some miracle you do happen to wedge in a word or two, they sit there nodding like a bobblehead on cocaine, waiting to jump back in with a detailed account of a fascinating topic such as their recent gallbladder surgery. It's impossible to have a meaningful exchange with someone who's hell-bent on delivering a soliloquy, and I don't care how good-hearted they might be, dominating every conversation is just rude.

The dream killer. While I was writing my first book, I'd occasionally meet with a friend who never missed an opportunity to express his doubt about the success of my project. "I hate to see you get your hopes up," he once told me. *He hates to see me get my hopes up?* That guy could take me from elation to deflation in a flash.

There's a lesson here for all of us who are working on artistic pursuits or any type of goal more ambitious than what the average person strives for: We have to be careful who we hang with. Rejection is a strong possibility whenever we put ourselves out there, and we don't need our friends or relatives shitting on our aspirations with doubt and negativity. I'm not saying these are bad people; they just don't get it. They don't get *you*. And I'm willing to bet they either have no ambitions themselves, or just as likely, they did at one time and someone (probably their parents, sorry to say) rewarded them with the same skepticism they're now passing on to us.

We can't expect these people to be a source of encouragement, so rather than risk having to defend your dreams, it's best to not even bring them up. Restrict the conversation to the weather. Share your successes and challenges with the kindred spirits in your tribe instead.

ଛଓ

Do Want You Want

People who bring you joy feed your spirit; the types I've just described deplete it. If you find yourself saying, "Well, Jeff is Jeff…" or "You know how Becky is…" you're recognizing obnoxious behavior, and if you continue to put up with it, you're enabling it. If someone continually drains your energy or insists on assaulting you with their negativity, give yourself permission to back away from that relationship. Let it fizzle out.

Sometimes we hang on to people out of habit or a perceived sense of loyalty because we've known them forever. Or because they're family. You can still stand up for yourself. Set boundaries. Tell your "Yeah, but…" friend who continually whines about the same issues something like, "Jen, you've been struggling with this for quite a while. What else do you have going on?" You can call someone on their behavior and still be kind.

ഌന

As you go about your day, be on the lookout for the joy in activities, in people, in things, and in nature that you can add to your list. Look for joy at work. Think of how you can be a source of joy to other people, especially those who don't seem to have much in their lives.

Buy a little notebook and at the end of each day, write down all the good things that happened, no matter how small. If someone buys you lunch, holds the door for you or pays you a compliment, record that in your notebook. Doing this will fill your subconscious with a pleasant feeling before you go to sleep, and when you're feeling down, you can refer to your notebook as a reminder of all the goodness that comes your way and your commitment to living with joy.

When you're driven by joy, you experience life differently. You project an upbeat spirit and emit a vibe that says, "Life is good." You easily see the humor that surrounds you. People are drawn to you, and they like you. This is important because other people, including those you have yet to meet, are also going to play a role in your adventure. Years ago, I decided to make joy my baseline state of being, and I know first-hand that it's a happy and fun as hell way to live!

3. Define Your Personal Brand

WHILE WE'RE USED TO hearing about branding in the context of businesses, the concept of a personal brand is relatively new. I've been training people on this topic only within the past ten years; it wasn't a thing back in my early days in outplacement. I can't say I love the words "personal brand." People aren't cattle and the term primarily reflects one's attributes in the context of what they do for work, not who they are in their personal life, but we'll go with it for now.

I begin my personal branding workshops by asking participants to call out a company with a strong corporate brand. In almost every session, somebody mentions Apple.

"What comes to mind when we think of Apple?" I ask.

They respond by naming Apple products—particularly the iPhone and iPad. They mention how easy they are to use and the cutting-edge technology behind them. They also mention the late Steve Jobs, the image of an apple with a bite out of it, and the color white.

Do Want You Want

Coca-Cola is another company that often comes up, along with the key characteristics of that brand: the signature soft drink and the words *Coca-Cola* in white script typeface on the red background. Older participants remember the "Things go better with Coke" slogan and the "I'd Like to Teach the World to Sing" song from the ads in the 1970s.

But what do we mean by a brand, anyway?

> **A brand is the combination of attributes that come together to form an impression in somebody's mind.**

It's not defined by a single characteristic. A brand could be comprised of the company's products, logo, slogan, spokesperson, leadership, philanthropy, and reputation in the industry. A brand can conjure colors, images, songs, and feelings.

Similar to how companies have brands, individuals have brands as well. You all have your own unique personal brand made up of characteristics that collectively form an impression and emit a vibe. Don't think personal brands only apply to people in the corporate world. Students, retirees, and even children have their own personal brands.

Let's look at the attributes of the personal brands of some celebrities. If I ask what comes to mind when you think of Oprah, you might rattle off her TV show, her OWN network, her struggle with weight loss and her role as a spokesperson with Weight Watchers, her humble beginnings, her book club, Stedman, her pal Gayle King, her spirituality and sense of fairness, her philanthropy, and more. The attributes of a personal brand might include the individual's body of work, their looks, their personality, their convictions, their associations, and other characteristics that make them who they are.

Would you say Oprah is an example of someone with a positive brand? She has both haters and a lot of people who think highly of her. You might consider her brand to be positive and someone else might not. That's just how it goes; the impression a brand conveys is subjective.

How about Kim Kardashian? Most people in my workshops groan when her name comes up. "What's her talent, again?" they ask. Others respect the empire she's built and consider her to be a role model for young women. Personally, I'm not thrilled that she's made big butts fashionable after I've spent half my life suffering through *Buns of Steel* videos to make mine smaller, but I'm sure many women would thank her for that.

It's possible to have more than one personal brand. I do; I have two separate brands under two different names. While I'm the same person, my author and comedian brand, Linda Lou, is a little too beer-drinkin', foul-mouthed, and politically incorrect for the corporate world, where I'm currently known as Linda Molony. (The last name changes with every husband.) The Linda Molony brand you see on LinkedIn projects a different image from my "anything goes" Linda Lou brand on Facebook.

Both corporate and personal brands are fluid; they're not set in stone. Brands can go from negative to positive, and positive to negative and back again. Angelina Jolie seemed a little cuckoo back when she was wearing a vial of Billy Bob Thornton's blood around her neck, but then she morphed into a United Nations Goodwill ambassador and an earth mother devoted to her six kids. We've seen the brands of numerous public figures change over time, including a wave of high-profile men whose brands are probably shot to hell forever due to indiscretions of a sexual nature. I will literally die of shock if we ever again see Matt Lauer regarded as a trusted news anchor.

I imagine how the scene would play out if my father came back to life and I had to catch him up on the world today. "You remember Bruce Jenner, Dad? Yeah... you'd better sit down." Now there's an example of the death of one brand—and an iconic one at that—and the emergence of another completely, and I mean *completely*, different brand. I love it. But I'm sad that some people have had to wait an awful long time just to be themselves.

So you see, brands can stay pretty stable or they can change—sometimes dramatically—or they can even die. Just as we never see the same river twice because it's always flowing, we never see the same people twice, either. Everyone is continuously learning and growing. Over time your personal brand will evolve, just as you do.

Benefits of determining your personal brand

Most people have no idea what their personal brand is, or that they even have one. That's too bad, because there are significant advantages to determining, building, communicating, and protecting your brand.

You project confidence. When you know what your brand is, and love it, you can't help but be more comfortable in your own skin. This changes you; you become more sure of yourself and you're less likely to care what other people think. You claim your personal power, and others view you in a more powerful way as well.

People are more likely to have an accurate impression of you. Once you've identified your personal brand, you know how you want to come across. You mindfully project certain aspects of what you're all about. You build your reputation with intention.

You distinguish yourself from your competitors. It's a safe bet that the people you'll be competing against for a job or a promotion will not have taken the time to determine their personal brand. This, along with the other self-assessment work you'll be doing, gives you a huge advantage since almost every aspect of the job search process requires a solid understanding of who you are and what you have to offer to a prospective employer.

Exercise: How to determine your personal brand

IMPORTANT: Please, *please* do the work in this chapter. It won't take long, and believe me, you'll be happy you did. As with all the exercises in this book, not everything is going to come to you in one sitting, so come back often and add to what you've done.

Now let's start putting your brand together. You'll see a blank worksheet on page 35; you can use my completed worksheet on page 34 as a guide. Here's how to fill it in:

Box 1 – Personality: List as many adjectives as you can that describe your personality. How do you think (or hope) you come across to people? You can see from my worksheet that I imagine myself as caring, funny, outgoing, approachable, and positive. I'm also picky, judgmental, and stubborn. (There's a reason I'm on my third husband.) Add a few non-flattering aspects of your personality in this box as well to keep yourself honest.

Boxes 2, 3, 4, and 5 – Skills: Title each of these boxes with your strongest skills. What do you feel most confident doing? What do people compliment you on? What could you teach others to do or what could you write an article about? It's okay if you're not using a skill in your current position or if you've developed it outside of work—it's still an area of ability.

Don't just name the skill and move on. Dig deeper into the details. For example, I listed "Writing" as a skill in Box 2, but I didn't stop there; I identified *what* I can write. As a technical writer, I can write resumes, software documentation, user manuals, proposals, website content, and promotional materials. Creatively, I write comedy, essays, non-fiction stories, and books. My point is, I drilled down into the details of my writing skills. I've done the same in Boxes 3, 4, and 5 for my training, career/life counseling, and public speaking skills.

List the things you know you do well, but only if you enjoy doing them. They are not necessarily one and the same. Many of us have items in our skill set that we never want to do again. I've gotten positive feedback on my ability to manage a staff, but I pray that kind of work is behind me. I know that's surprising considering how much I love to tell everyone what to do, but I can barely keep myself in line much less other people.

Box 6 – Knowledge: Make a list of everything you know something about, whether or not it's related to work. Maybe you avidly read about nutrition, or you've learned a lot about karate or gardening. Again, think of subjects you could teach or write about. The things you list here should be different from what you have in Boxes 2, 3, 4, and 5.

Box 7 – Niche: In this box, show what makes you unique. How are you different from other people who do the same type of job? What do you know that they don't seem to? What different perspective do you have? How are you weird? What's your freaky superpower? How does it work to your benefit? I'm weird in that I'm super down-to-earth and way too fun for most business settings, but it works to my benefit because people seem to pick up on my authentic nature and trust me.

DO WANT YOU WANT

Determine Your Personal Brand (Linda's worksheet)	
1. Personality	**2. Skill: Writing**
Caring Funny Outgoing Approachable Positive Picky Judgmental Stubborn	Technical writing: websites, proposals, resumes, articles, white papers, software documentation, user manuals, website content, promotional materials Creative writing: comedy, essays, non-fiction stories, books, speeches, obituaries, dating profiles, LinkedIn profiles Communicate technical information to non-technical audiences Good eye for structure and layout
3. Skill: Training	**4. Skill: Career/Life Counseling**
Design training programs Deliver training (classroom and virtual) in an engaging, down-to-earth manner Create instructional materials Assess training needs Evaluate training effectiveness	Help people assess their strengths, identify priorities, explore options, determine optimal path Help with their communication strategy Instill confidence and motivate people to keep going Keep people on track of their goals
5. Skill: Public Speaking	**6. Additional Areas of Knowledge**
Stand-up comedy Training (classroom and virtual) TV segments Radio (former announcer) On-stage storytelling	Yoga (former instructor) Self-esteem Hospice care (former volunteer) Personal finance Book publishing Dance – ballet, Zumba, jazz
7. Niche	
I'm super down-to-earth and way too fun for most business settings, but it works to my benefit in that people pick up on my authentic nature and trust me. I can make people feel at ease when they are going through difficult situations.	

Chapter 3. Define Your Personal Brand

Determine Your Personal Brand	
1. **Personality**	2. **Skill:**
3. **Skill:**	4. **Skill:**
5. **Skill:**	6. **Additional Areas of Knowledge**
7. **Niche**	

DO WANT YOU WANT

Before we go any further, take a look at everything on your worksheet. Do you like what you see? Are you proud of those words? If not, what needs to change? Take out whatever doesn't ring true to you. Keep modifying it until you're happy with what you see. You can always change it as you get more clarity about yourself.

Exercise: Write your personal branding statement

Now we're going to take the information you've collected about yourself and condense it into a single statement that encapsulates what your brand is all about. Don't freak out. This isn't as hard as you might think.

Here is my branding statement based on what I came up with on the worksheet. I couldn't integrate every single thing I listed into one sentence—that would be impossible—but you can see this is pretty much the gist of what I'm all about.

Linda's personal branding statement
"I am a kind, funny, and down-to-earth career strategist with expertise in writing, training, and motivating others to achieve their personal and professional goals."

The template below shows my approach to how I did this.

Personal branding statement TEMPLATE
"I am a (personality characteristic from Box 1), (another personality characteristic), and (one more personality characteristic) (what you are) with expertise in (skill from Box 2, 3, 4, or 5), (another skill), and (one more skill) to (beneficial outcome)."

Now it's your turn to write your personal branding statement. To make things easy, be sure to use this template and don't deviate from this formula. All you have to do is plug your information into the parentheses. Did you ever play Mad Libs when you were a kid? It's kind of like that.

CHAPTER 3. DEFINE YOUR PERSONAL BRAND

Your personal branding statement

Feeling stuck? Maybe these examples will help.

Sample personal branding statement
"I am a driven, energetic, and profit-focused production manager with expertise in operational efficiency, fiscal oversight, and leading teams to drive financial performance."

You can modify this formula if you're not yet sure "what you are" or if you want to explore a new career direction.

Sample "not sure what you are" personal branding statement
"I am a kind, compassionate, and positive service-oriented professional open to a new opportunity in customer relations, office management, and client communication."

As I mentioned before, people not in the workforce still have a personal brand, and this formula works for them as well.

Sample "not in workforce" personal branding statement
"I am an engaging, vibrant, and confident retired teacher who is looking to have as much fun as possible in my remaining years on earth."

Please don't continue without at least taking a stab at this. As with every other exercise in this book, you can't make a mistake. Nothing is set in stone.

Do Want You Want

Keep in mind that you are the primary audience for your branding statement; you're telling yourself this is how you want the world to see you. This is the impression you'd like to give. But there is a secondary audience: people you meet.

The reason I advise you to stick to the template is because all but the first part of your branding statement serves another purpose. If I delete the personality characteristics from my branding statement, I'm left with "I am a career strategist with expertise in writing, training, and motivating others to achieve their personal and professional goals." This is a nice, ten-second intro I can use if someone asks, "So Linda, what do you do?"

Do you see the method behind the madness?

Once you have it written, test your branding statement by running it by people who know you. Share your worksheet as well. Your friends and colleagues may bring up skills or personality traits that you hadn't thought about.

I test my branding statement every time I do a workshop. Before I begin, I ask people to write down three adjectives that they feel describe me, even if they're seeing me for the first time and have had only a few minutes to form any kind of opinion. After we get to the part where they share their branding statements, I have them pull out those three words. They almost always say things like "enthusiastic," "approachable," "energetic," or "outgoing." That's what I want to hear—that means I'm coming across the way I want to. I'd worry if they'd written "standoffish," "reserved" or "intimidating."

Exuding your brand

Note that we don't verbalize our personality characteristics in our ten-second intro. I would never introduce myself by saying, "Hi, I'm a funny, kind, and down-to-earth career strategist…" We leave those personality traits off our ten-second introduction because we *exude* them.

Whether we do it intentionally or not, we're always giving off a vibe that communicates something about us and we don't even have to say a word. One way we exude nonverbal cues is through facial expressions. We've all met someone and immediately concluded *I don't like his stinkin' looks*. We probably picked up on a raised eyebrow or a chin held a bit too high, which we interpret as a sense of arrogance or superiority. Conversely, we've all met someone we loved right off the bat because of their pleasant expression and twinkling eyes.

If I want people to think of me as "kind, funny and down-to-earth," I need to exude those qualities. This means I should assume an open posture, offer a welcoming smile, make good eye contact, and have a pleasing baseline expression as opposed to the resting bitch face I catch myself making when I'm scrutinizing something on my phone.

Take a look at the three personality traits you've chosen to include in your branding statement. What does someone who exudes those qualities look like? Do you exude those qualities?

In addition to posture and facial expressions, you exude your brand through your personal style. This includes your hairstyle, your clothing, and your choice of accessories such as jewelry, purses, and eyeglasses. They all say something about your personal brand. Think of a chemical engineer and then think of an art teacher. Note the different images you conjured in your mind's eye.

When you're shopping, make sure whatever you buy aligns with your brand. If you buy only what brings you joy, whatever you purchase will reflect the "real" you. Therefore, what you exude will be an accurate representation of who you are and the impression you wish to give.

Exercise: Where do you hit a home run?

Now let's identify what you do better than ninety-nine percent of all the people on earth, or where you "hit a home run." This is what you can do with the confidence that makes you say, "Hold my beer. I got this."

Identify five areas where you feel you hit a home run. As I did in my example on the next page, give as many details as possible. Don't be afraid to toot your own horn. If you can't come up with five right now, write down what comes to mind and come back to this exercise some other time.

Where I Hit a Home Run (Linda's example)
Area #1: I'm a super engaging trainer.
I *love* to train people, and even if the training content is boring as hell, I'll find a way to have fun with it. I integrate humor into my sessions, but I ensure that real, measurable learning takes place. I'm thrilled when I see people come into a training with apprehension and leave feeling empowered and confident.
Area #2: I'm a great resume writer.
I fancy myself to be in the top five percent of resume writers on earth. I know how to dig into and pull out the important aspects of a person's background and present their value in the way that will best support their objective. I can make people look amazing without writing a word of fiction, and I love that they feel much more confident presenting themselves to a prospective employer. I can even make this process fun.
Area #3: I'm a skilled wordsmith.
I can write just about anything. I am a skilled wordsmith and have a good eye for document design and layout. I can synthesize complex information (even if I don't fully understand it myself) and present it in a way that's easily understood by the intended audience
Area #4: I make people feel at ease.
I make people feel at ease, particularly when they're going through a stressful time. I have a lot of experience working with people who've just lost their jobs and I was a hospice volunteer for years, providing comfort to dying people and their families. I am a bit self-deprecating and have a down-to-earth communication style that radiates honesty. People feel they can be themselves around me. They trust me and can sense that I have their best interest at heart.
Area #5: I'm funny.
I can see humor in almost anything and I know how to use it appropriately. I'm somehow able to keep the inappropriate humor to myself even if it's freakin' hilarious, as most inappropriate humor is.

CHAPTER 3. DEFINE YOUR PERSONAL BRAND

Where I Hit a Home Run
Area #1:
Area #2:.
Area #3:
Area #4:
Area #5:

Review what you've written. If you've identified any new skills that you forgot to include on the branding worksheet, add them now. If you need to adjust your personal branding statement, do that, too.

Do Want You Want

The benefits of kicking ass

Now that you know what you do best, go balls to the wall with it. Sharpen those skills and get better and better. Why? Because when you kick ass at what you do, you'll reap these benefits:

You're recognized as a valuable asset to the organization. People regard you as an expert. You're the go-to person when someone has questions and you're the one who saves the day when there's a major problem. This puts you in a good position to negotiate for more money, and you don't necessarily have to wait for your next salary review. You're treated well because they don't want you to jump ship. You build job security (as if there is such a thing) since you're less likely to be targeted when the company prepares for a staff reduction.

People leave you alone. You've built a reputation for getting the job done and you do it well. Nobody tells you what to do or how to do it. You're allowed to work on your own terms without anyone hovering over you or monitoring your activity. People respect your time and the boundaries you set, and that is a beautiful feeling.

You're allowed to be the "real" you. The more amazing you are at what you do, the less you have to edit yourself and the more you're allowed to express your individuality. My office in my last job was like "the Linda museum." Everything I looked at brought me joy: my funky artwork, my healing crystals, my little "Well behaved women have no fun" sign on my desk that a client gave me, my calendar of colorful outhouses in the woods. I'm sure every time my boss looked at my Helen Keller bobblehead he thought, "Good God, Linda is a freak!" But he knew the clients loved me (and my office) and nobody could write resumes or design workshops or put together a proposal like I could, so what was he gonna do?

※

You need to recognize what's in your home run zone because that's where you want to be spending your time. That's where you're going to have the most fun, and because you'll be using the talents that come naturally to you, that's also where you'll make the most money. And money is important—it pays for the things that bring you joy.

Exercise: Write a personal mission statement

Businesses and non-profit organizations have written mission statements, and it's good for individuals to have them, too. Of course, hardly anyone has actually taken the time to figure theirs out, but you're different.

Your personal mission statement articulates your purpose in life, meaning whatever you think it is at this time. My mission statement came to me out of nowhere one morning back in 2003 during my yoga practice. I jumped out of my downward dog and immediately wrote it down.

Linda's Personal Mission Statement
"To help people access, acknowledge, and accept their innate talents and to help them share those talents with the world."

When I looked at what I'd written, I knew I was seeing the truth. I understood why I'd always loved working in outplacement—that type of work aligns perfectly with my life's mission. I love to help people find their direction based on their talents, interests, and values. I love helping them communicate what they have to offer, both verbally and in writing, and then helping them get their talents out to the people and organizations that need them. Helping people discover how to be their best and supporting them along the way is central to who I am.

You can see how my work in career development aligns with my life's mission, and how my life's mission aligns with what I know about and where I hit a home run. That's no coincidence! After I defined my life's mission, I understood why I was miserable in some of the tech writing jobs I've held. Sure, I was putting my skills to use, but I didn't feel I was helping anybody who would directly benefit from my efforts.

I wish I could tell people in my workshops, "I'm gonna give you fifteen minutes to think about the purpose of your existence, articulate it succinctly, and then everyone will share their personal mission statement with the group." If only it were that easy. I also wish I could give you a formula to follow, as I did with your personal branding statement. You can see how I structured my mission statement, but the structure of yours will probably be completely different.

DO WANT YOU WANT

If you have an idea of what your life's mission might be, go ahead and write it here.

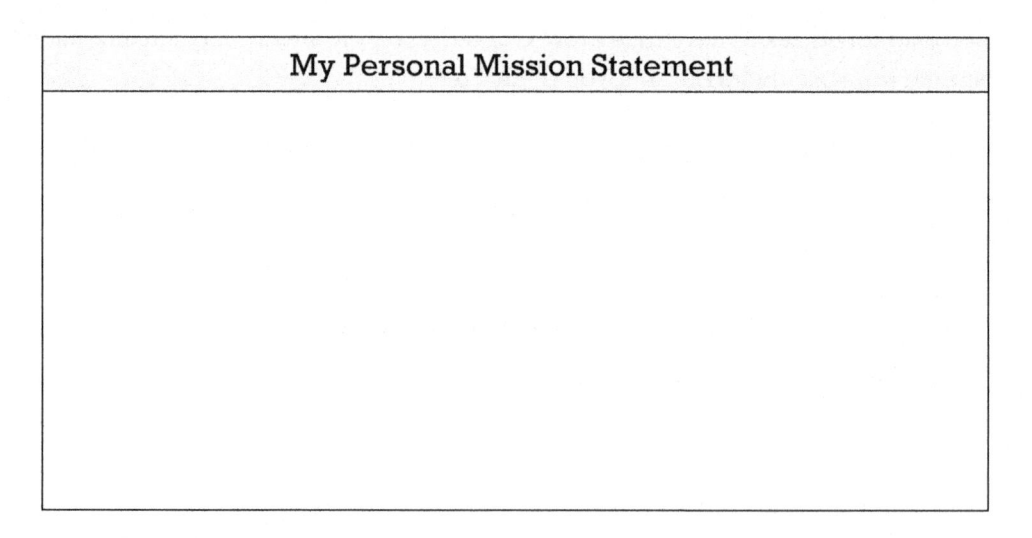

My Personal Mission Statement

If it's not coming to you, at least start thinking about it. At some point it will hit you, probably when you least expect it, like when you're in the shower or in line at the grocery store. When you do have that *a-ha!* moment, stop the world and get that thing on paper. Otherwise, you'll lose it.

Exercise: A few more questions

I'm glad you're doing all this work, and trust me when I say you'll be glad, too. You know the type of person you are and the talents you have to offer. You probably have some ideas about how you want to present yourself on a resume, and you're prepared to respond to typical interview questions such as "What strengths would you bring to this position?" and "How would your coworkers describe your personality?"

Before we wind up, I have just a few more questions. Don't just read each one and continue on—write out your answers.

CHAPTER 3. DEFINE YOUR PERSONAL BRAND

- What did you want to be when you were a kid? Does anything about that still interest you?

- If you didn't have to work, how would you spend your time? What would a typical day look like?

- What would you like to learn about that's unrelated to the work you do now?

- Suppose that for whatever reason, you had to change careers. What's your Plan B?

DO WANT YOU WANT

- What part of your life would you like to change? Where do you seem out of balance? What could go better?

- What do you need?

- What's your biggest concern right now?

- How well do you handle stress?

- How important is job security? (Spoiler alert: unless you're a Supreme Court justice, there's no such thing.)

- What values at the heart of your character *must* be aligned with what you do at work?

4. Plot Your Direction

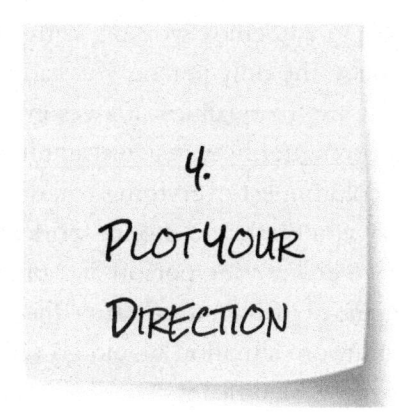

THE EXERCISES IN THIS CHAPTER will help you gain clarity on possible directions to pursue, including some ideas for a side hustle or what you might do just for fun. I think you'll find these exercises will prove to be invaluable, especially when you're ready to evaluate opportunities.

Exercise: Likes and Dislikes

This is a simple, yet powerful, exercise to help you identify the conditions that work and don't work for you in a job.

Notice the left side of the worksheet is labeled "Likes" and the right side is labeled "Dislikes." On the left side of the page, starting with your current position, make a list of everything you like about that job. (If you're not working right now, start with your most recent position.) Just as you did with the personal branding exercises, give details. If you enjoy working with the person you report to, don't just write, "Good boss." What exactly makes a good boss? Someone who's eager to share their knowledge? Allows you to work autonomously and never breathes down your neck? Doesn't care what time you come in or how you do your job as long as you get it done?

Jot down everything you can think of that you like about working there. Consider the company culture, the benefits package, the commute, and the work you do. Again, be specific. What exactly do you like about it? Do you have a variety of responsibilities? Do you enjoy working with the public or are you self-aware enough to know you're the only person you can truly stand? Do you have awesome coworkers? What are the qualities of awesome coworkers? Write down whatever comes to mind, no matter how insignificant it might seem.

Then in the Dislikes column, list everything you don't like about that job, no matter how minor or crazy you think it is. I once worked for a company that had fifty employees and only two unisex, one-person-at-a-time bathrooms. To this day, I am nauseated by the memory of the stench after the CEO did his business on Taco Tuesday. So that bathroom situation would go on my Dislike side. Call me crazy, but to me that was pretty significant.

After you're done listing all the Likes and Dislikes for your current or most recent position, draw a line across the page and do the same for the job you held before that. Then do the same for the job before that, and the job before that. Fill the entire page, even if you go back to jobs you held in high school. Count volunteer work, too.

Likes	Dislikes

Do Want You Want

Likes	Dislikes

Now review everything you've written. What patterns do you see? I'm sure you already had an idea in the back of your mind of what you've liked and haven't liked about different jobs, but writing these things down and seeing the patterns that emerge bring this information to the forefront of your mind and gives you clarity on what to look for, and avoid, in your next position.

The Likes and Dislikes exercise can be used in a variety of scenarios. For example, if you're looking for a place to live and are considering different housing options, this approach can help determine your next move. You can also use this to clarify what's important to you in a major purchase such as a new car. If you're single, this will help you identify the type of person that's right for you, and not so right, by assessing how things have gone with previous partners. Had I considered my relationship Likes and Dislikes after my first divorce, I might have spared myself my second marriage and a couple of other dubious relationships. (Kidding—they all have contributed in some way to who I am today. But still…)

Exercise: Your preferred working conditions

Now we're going to define the conditions in a job that need to be in place for you to enjoy life. Refer to your Likes/Dislikes worksheet as you consider each of the following.

The work itself. You'll be happiest, and will probably make the most money, when your work is aligned with your life's mission and allows you to showcase the skills in your home run zone.

- What would you like to be doing in the course of a day? What type of work brings you joy? Be specific.

The leadership style of the person you report to. The person you report to can make or break your happiness on the job. Every other work condition can be perfect, but your spirit will be broken if you have to answer to someone you can't stand. I truly believe that one of your primary responsibilities is to make sure the boss-person looks good. That's hard to do if you don't like or respect them.

- What are the qualities of the best boss you ever had?

- What type of leader motivates you to give it your all and make that person look good?

- Do you prefer to be given a lot of direction and ongoing support, or do you prefer to be left alone once the expectations are clear?

Opportunity to advance in your current path and learn more. Whether or not you're driven to climb the corporate ladder is up to you. Traditionally the "Type A careerist" has been the measure of success, but the only thing that matters is how *you* define success. Maybe your life's mission is tied to what you do outside of work and your job serves no other purpose than to put food on the table. Maybe you're developing a side hustle that you hope will someday be your primary source of income and your job is paying the bills until then.

I have plenty of comedian and musician friends whose passion lies in their creative work and they have day jobs only to get by. I've worked with executives and other professionals who, after working their asses off for years, wanted to downshift into a less demanding position. Who could blame them?

- Are you constantly eyeing your next role and positioning yourself to move forward in your career? Or does the thought of taking on more responsibility seem like a nightmare?

- If it's important to you to advance in your current path, what does that path look like?

- Considering your desired career path, what job-related skills would you like to improve?

- What new skills could you acquire that might elevate you to the next step in your career?

- Would you take advantage of employer-funded certifications and tuition reimbursement for continuing education classes that would help you get ahead?

The organizational culture. Company cultures can range from strictly business where everyone is all suited up and no one has cracked a smile in the past decade to the relaxed "work hard, play hard" environments where employees drink beer and play foosball in shorts and flip-flops in the break room. Most people prefer something in between.

Social expectations of a workplace vary as well. I once had a three-month technical writing gig at a health insurance company where I swear every week a collection was going around for somebody's wedding shower or new baby, or I was getting hit up to buy candy bars so somebody's kid could go to cheer camp. One afternoon I got an email from a fellow member of my "team" asking for a fifty-dollar contribution toward a birthday present for the department manager. This was a woman who clearly did not like my stinkin' looks. She could barely suppress a throw-up burp when she walked by my cubicle, so no way would I fork out fifty, I repeat, *fifty* dollars so she could enjoy a luxurious day at the spa. I politely declined. The Friday before her birthday weekend, she called a meeting to go over our project status. But first, the "team" presented her with a glittery gift bag and a card signed by four out of the five people in the room whose wallets were fifty bucks lighter. She dramatically gushed over (almost) everyone's generosity and obvious adoration for her leadership and then shot me her signature puke-in-the-back-of-her-throat look.

Don't get me wrong. I've met some of my dearest friends in the workplace. Forming friendships with coworkers can not only increase your happiness on the job, but preserve your sanity. But there's a big difference between the natural progression of work relationships and a culture that more or less imposes forced participation.

- What type of work culture are you most comfortable in?

- What would you prefer to wear to work?

- How do you feel about social obligations in the workplace? Do you enjoy attending, or organizing, work-related events or do you prefer to stay as far away from that stuff as possible?

- Do you enjoy having a close "work family" or are you content as an outsider?

Company size. Both large and small organizations have their benefits and downsides. In a small company, you typically get to wear more hats since there are fewer people to get things done. You'll have more opportunities to do and learn different things, and if you're an idea person who's always coming up with better ways to get things done, you'll find it easier to implement new processes in a smaller company that doesn't make you go through layers of approval.

One of the things I loved about working in a small company was that we received ongoing feedback on how we were doing instead of having to endure a formal performance evaluation, commonly known as the "shit sandwich." You may be familiar with the "You're doing great, but you kind of suck at these things, but overall, you're doing great" structure of those tortuous meetings, which are particularly loathsome when led by someone with the "I don't give anybody a five out of five" leadership philosophy.

In contrast, larger companies typically have clearly defined processes, roles, and escalation paths in place in order to ensure consistency. Companies with more employees generally have more resources, offer more opportunities for advancement or relocation, and generally provide higher salaries and comprehensive benefits.

- Do you prefer the structure of a larger organization or does a smaller company appeal to you more? Why?

The physical environment. This is a tough one, especially if you're like me and are annoyed by just about everything. I go bonkers if I hear a radio playing music I don't like, I'm particular about lighting, I need windows, I don't like to be cold, and we've already discussed the bathroom situation.

- How about you? What physical environment do you work best in?

Remote, in-office, or a combination? Maybe your optimal environment is home, sweet home. Working from home is fantastic—you can roll out of bed, grab your coffee, and fire up the workstation in your pajamas. There's no commute, you can go out for a run at lunch, throw in a load of laundry, put the roast in the oven… what's not to love?

Well, remote work might be tough if you don't have a dedicated workspace at home or if you live for social interaction. And if you're not comfortable figuring out technology glitches on your own, you'll miss being able to pop into a coworker's cubicle for help.

Once considered a luxury that we practically had to beg for, working remotely has become, if only by necessity, more widely accepted by employers. We'll probably continue to see a shift toward telecommuting in industries where it's possible. Is working remotely for you, though?

- Would you prefer to work entirely at home, entirely onsite, or a combination of the two?

Part-time work. The majority of part-time positions pay hourly rates that are close to minimum wage, but depending on your skill set and industry, you may be able to find high-paying part-time employment opportunities. It's rare to find part-time work that offers benefits, but that's not to say it's impossible. For most people, the option to work part-time is determined by their financial picture. We'll talk more about that later.

- Is working part-time an option for you right now? Is it a goal you may want to set for the future?

Temporary and contract work. This category of work encompasses a broad range of levels of expertise, with assignments lasting from a single day to several months.

Some temporary positions don't require a lot of training, as when an office hires a temporary receptionist to fill in while someone is sick or on vacation. I was introduced to the field of corporate outplacement through such a temp position. I had quit a management position in a god-awful, exclusively female non-profit where I learned how petty and backstabbing the ladies can be when no men are around to witness the drama. I left without having another job lined up, so to have some money coming in while I figured out my next step, I marched my ass to a temporary employment agency. "Just make me a receptionist somewhere," I told them. They placed me in a small company providing corporate outplacement services. I had no idea what outplacement was, or that a two-week temporary assignment would lead to the most rewarding work of my career. By noon on my first day, the owner of the company could tell what I really had to offer and soon I was writing resumes and helping clients with their job search. I stayed with that firm for almost three years before I left to attend grad school.

In another type of contract work, individuals are hired because a company needs their particular area of expertise, usually to help with a specific project and usually for a pre-determined amount of time. It's easiest to find these types of contract opportunities through a staffing firm specializing in professional services. Some offer paid benefits, though that's generally not the case.

Over the years, I've had several contract training and tech writing gigs that lasted from a few months to more than two years. Some were on a W-2 basis, where I received a weekly or biweekly paycheck with taxes and Social Security taken out. I've also worked a couple of jobs as an independent contractor, which is a form of self-employment. When working on a 1099 basis, your client company pays your hourly rate and you are responsible for withholding and paying your own income and self-employment taxes (Social Security and Medicare taxes). With this arrangement, you're responsible for paying one hundred percent of your Social Security tax; in a W-2 structure, half is paid by the employer or contracting agency. This is one of the reasons why, as an independent contractor, you ask for a higher rate.

Personally, I loved contract work, maybe because I have deep-seeded commitment issues. I like the idea of being somewhere for a finite amount of time and then it's over. If you have a crappy day at work or have to report to a throw-up-burp department head, who cares? In a matter of time that place will be history.

By doing contract work, you gain exposure to a variety of industries and work processes. You're always learning something new. You get paid by the hour, so you can fly out of there like Fred Flintstone when the five o'clock whistle blows. I love the fact that you're there strictly to work; they've hired you only for the skills you're bringing to the party. This presents a great opportunity to showcase your talents, and as I've said before, when you kick ass at what you do, you get to be your authentic self.

As a contractor, you sit on the periphery of the workplace culture, so you're spared the office politics. You don't have to try too hard to fit in. I was a total oddball in some companies, but you know what? I think some people regarded me as a breath of fresh air. Because I was an objective outsider, I could raise concerns at the conference table that might have been too risky for an employee to bring up. People trusted me; I wasn't a threat to them. I wasn't after their job or trying to position myself for a promotion. I was just me being me, trying to do a good job until I could go back home to my sacred space.

Even though I wasn't a "real" employee, I met some of my dearest friends at contract gigs. My friend Donna had a big job with an office across from my cubicle at the throw-up burp place. At first I thought she was a lunatic because every morning I could hear her randomly laughing in there all by herself. Then one day I heard Robin Quivers' theme music. I peeked in and asked, "Are you listening to Howard Stern?" That's all it took to be bonded for life.

I think the nature of contract work motivates you to do an incredible job, especially if you like the gig and hope your contract gets extended, as often will happen. When your role in the project is completed, you'll want the company to report positive feedback about your work to the staffing agency so they'll have the confidence to place you somewhere else.

CHAPTER 4. PLOT YOUR DIRECTION

Often a contract gig leads to an offer of full-time employment. In fact, some companies prefer initially to engage individuals on a contract basis to make sure the person is a fit with their needs and culture. This is a win-win situation; both parties have a good idea of what they're getting into before making a more permanent commitment. Kind of like living together before tying the knot. Since there are no guarantees, you'd be wise to view contract work as a way to provide a temporary flow of money, with the probability that you'll be hitting the streets again once the gig is up. Still, you can always ask about the likelihood of the contract being extended.

- Do you learn quickly and easily adapt to new work environments?

- Do you have the risk tolerance and financial stability to consider contract work?

5. Should I Stay or Should I Go?

IF YOU'RE HAPPY WITH YOUR JOB and wouldn't change a thing, consider yourself lucky. Most people wish they could feel that way. For you the question is, what can you do to love your job even more?

If that's the case, continue to be a rock star and keep hitting those home runs. Learn everything you can to support your professional development. Position yourself to be as valuable as possible, but don't let yourself be taken advantage of, by either your colleagues or your company's leadership. The reward for good work is more work, and that can lead to burnout. Be sure to maintain balance with other aspects of your life. Set and work toward some professional goals, as well as personal goals that will bring you joy and a sense of accomplishment. They are equally important.

Good reasons to stay in a job you can't wait to get out of

Being miserable in your job is an awful feeling, and that misery is sure to permeate other aspects of your life as well. But sometimes the wisest thing to do is to stay.

If any of the following ring true for you, consider hanging in there a little while longer.

- You need to reach a certain milestone before you can retire or you'll lose a significant amount of money.
- You need to stay long enough to cash in on a hefty bonus.
- You have good reason to believe a layoff is coming and if you hold out, chances are you'll score a generous separation package.
- Your financial obligations require the income you're currently bringing in and you don't think you'll see that kind of money if you make a move. (Double check this. Are you sure your compensation is more than what the market is paying in your area? Have you done the salary research or are you going by hearsay?)
- Your current job is a stepping-stone to another position in the company, and you expect that next position will bring you joy.
- You think the current suckiness is due to a temporary condition, after which you expect things will significantly improve.

Any one of these are reason enough to remain where you are. While you ride out your time, realize that you're staying put not because you have to, but because you want to. Your current job is the smartest place for you to be for now, the key words being "for now."

Periodically reassess the situation. You can't wait forever if you see no promotion in sight, or the layoff you were counting on lingers in an unspecified timeframe, or you have no real indication that your incompetent boss who's been hanging by a frayed thread is ever actually going to get canned.

How to survive until you can leave

Although you may feel like a prisoner marking each day on your calendar with a giant X, try your best to make life tolerable until your release. Continue to identify and develop your talents while you create a plan for what you're going to do with them. Focus on and work toward your goals. I can't stress that enough. In the meantime, maybe the following strategies will help preserve your mental health until you get out of the big house.

See how you can tweak your job to make it more tolerable. Take a look at what you have in the Dislike column in the Likes and Dislikes exercise. What's your biggest pain point? How can you alleviate that? If there's a particular aspect of your job that you can't stand doing, can it be moved onto someone else's plate? If the daily commute is taking years off your life, can you work from home a couple of days a week? If you're dying of boredom, is there a problem in the organization that you would enjoy solving? That would add a nice accomplishment to your resume.

One of the technical writing jobs I took when I first came to Las Vegas required everyone to be at work promptly at 7:00. Because of my lengthy morning beautification ritual, I had to set my alarm for the ungodly hour of 5:15. I always felt tired. I'd work on half a cylinder during the day, and at night I'd lie around like a slug watching TV or wasting time on the Internet. Back then I was still in the comedy open mic scene, trying to get in some stage time so someone might eventually give me a paid gig, but I almost never felt like going out, much less performing.

I asked if I could change my hours to a 9:00 start time, and that made a huge difference. I'd wake up before the alarm went off (that's always a personal victory) and had time to do an exercise video or work on some new comedy material before I left the house. I was able to do what's most important to me first. I also gained time at night; I could go to an open mic or to my favorite live music venue or stay up late writing at home without suffering the next day.

By making that one adjustment, I created a structure that enabled me to work on my personal pursuits. I felt a hundred times better since I was exercising regularly again, which in turn gave me more energy. I no longer resented having to sit in a cubicle all day. Overall, my quality of life improved significantly with a simple change of schedule.

What would it take to make your job more tolerable? Is there something you can tweak just a bit that would result in an amazing improvement? Make a case for it and develop a strategy to present your idea to the decision makers. The worst they can say is no, and if you don't ask, there's zero chance that anything will change.

Use your lunch hour constructively. If you enjoy shooting the breeze and having a laugh with your coworkers at lunch, that's fantastic. Keep that going.

Treasure the kindred spirits who share your work values. When I worked at GE, we *lived* for our lunch hour and felt rejuvenated when we returned to our desks. But if you're listening to some blowhard drone away about his new garage door opener while he shovels a tuna sandwich into his mouth, please choose to spend your time more wisely. Go out for a walk. Do something—*anything*—that will bring you closer to your goal of getting out of there. Work on a personal project that brings you joy. When I was writing my first book, I sat by myself in the lunchroom at the throw-up burp company almost every day and did some editing. People must have assumed I was super dedicated to work, the way I pored over my papers, and so they left me alone. Which was glorious. One guy did ask what I was doing. "Oh, I'm writing a book," I said. "It's called *Bastard Husband: A Love Story*." He tiptoed away.

Take comfort that no experience is ever wasted. Even though you don't enjoy what you're doing right now, chances are you're honing skills in your current position that are related to your ultimate goal. In my case, the technical writing and editing skills I developed at jobs I hated helped make my creative writing crisper. In technical writing, you're communicating to busy readers who want to do something or know something. They're not reading for fun; they want to get in and out of a document as quickly as possible so they can get on with their jobs. In comedy, you have to get from the setup to the punch line in as few words as possible; if you meander with details that have nothing to do with the laugh, the bit will fall flat. Technical writing and comedy writing require a similar economy of words. In each scenario, the content has to be expressed as succinctly as possible.

Similarly, writing and assembling giant technical proposals required the ability to structure a great deal of complex content in a way that made sense for my intended audience. I had to understand my readers and my purpose for writing. What did they need to know? What did they need to know *now*? What was the best way to present all that stuff?

That skill proved its value while I was writing my memoir. I had a lot of background information to weave in: where I came from, how I got to Las Vegas, why I thought it was a good idea to marry and move across the country with someone who got wicked obnoxious when he boozed it up. I had to determine what my audience needed to know, what they didn't need to know, and what they needed to know at that point in the book. Then I had to figure out how to weave in all the back story in a way that would keep the present story moving. At times I thought my head would explode, but because of my strong technical writing background, my brain could handle that task.

By writing boring proposals and software documentation for a company I truly did not give a crap about, I was also training my brain to hone the writing skills I *did* care about. When you frame what you're doing now in a way that supports where you ultimately want to be, your current situation becomes more tolerable. You resist it less.

Maybe you can't connect what you're doing today with how this experience will benefit you down the line. That's okay; trust there's something of value going on anyway. At some point you'll realize you had to go through *this* in order to do *that* better. Everything fits together in the big picture of life. The universe unfolds in divine order. Annoying to hear, but I do believe it.

Remind yourself of what *doesn't* suck about your job. Again, refer to your Likes and Dislikes exercise. What's in your Likes column? Focus on the positive and appreciate the good. Think about the worst job you ever had and, not to sound like a Pollyanna, be thankful you're not doing that. If you've ever been without a paycheck and found yourself in dire financial circumstances, appreciate how good it feels to have a regular source of income. Identify the value your job brings to your life today.

Keep things in perspective. By nature, some jobs must be taken very seriously, like if you're a brain surgeon or an airline pilot or a hairdresser. People's lives and self-esteem depend on you. Otherwise, you can lighten up.

Too often our unhappiness in a job stems from that fact that we care too much. We want our work culture to be pleasant. We want leadership to be fair and competent. Our standards are high; we have a strong work ethic and we want things to be done right. Sadly, sometimes we seem to care more than anyone else.

The truth is, not every workplace deserves your level of commitment. Sometimes everything around you is total bullshit, which is exactly why you're itching to break free. So instead of knocking yourself out and making yourself crazy, just commit to getting through the day with self-preservation as your only goal. Pretend there's such a thing as a workplace hospice where your sole objective is to make yourself comfortable and keep the pain to a minimum. Think of it as corporate palliative care. Just for fun, buy yourself some bendy sick-bed straws and every time you sip your drink during an interminable meeting, you'll remind yourself that you'll soon be in a better place.

Continue to do an amazing job. Even if you despise your job and everyone in it, never compromise the quality of what you do. Although I hated every minute sitting in cubicles at the throw-up-burp place and the office with the Taco Tuesday bathroom, I still created process documentation, user manuals, and proposals that were a goddamn work of art. Sometimes the people I reported to didn't have the brains to distinguish good documentation from bad; I could have produced a total piece of crap and they wouldn't have known the difference. But *I* would have known. **No matter how loathsome your current situation is, always do the best you can.**

Good reasons to leave a job ASAP

Staying in a job that crushes your soul takes its toll in a number of ways and can damage your self-esteem to the point where over time you may question whether you could even make it anywhere else. Don't let it get to that. Here are some good reasons to get your act together and prepare to say *adios*.

You have no work-life balance. We've talked about this quite a bit—you know what imbalance looks like. Your job seems to take up every waking moment. You're missing out on time with your kids, household projects remain half completed, and you can't remember when you last went to the gym. Even if you love what you do, it's not healthy for your job to be all-consuming.

Over the years I noticed my outplacement clients who had the toughest time coping with job loss were the ones who had put all their eggs in one basket: their job. When the job was gone, they had nothing. They completely lost their sense of self because their identity had been tied to what they do, not who they are. I didn't find them pleasant people to be around. They came across as bitter and resentful. They resisted any help and were skeptical of whatever assistance I had to offer. The fact that you've made it this far in this book tells me you know better.

Your job is starting to affect your health. This is what happens when the absence of work-life balance ascends to a new level.

Let me tell you a little story. I *loved* my last job. As you know, I loved working in corporate outplacement, which was intrinsically rewarding and aligned with my life's mission. I loved working for the owner of the company. He conducted business with integrity, was fair and appreciative of everything I did, and rewarded my efforts with an above-market salary and generous bonuses and vacation time. I was allowed to work about half the time at home and almost completely autonomously. He respected my opinions, and even if he disagreed, he would always give careful consideration to my input. I had an office with windows and a balcony, and I could decorate it with oddball things that brought me joy. The ladies room was gleaming and almost never in use. (I really don't have a bathroom problem; I just like a nice ladies room.)

So why would I leave this dream job? Well, as much as I loved the work, there was too much of it. I was sweating away nights, weekends… almost every waking moment. I found myself dreading the comedy gigs on my calendar. I'd scramble to put my set together, always wishing I had more time to polish it up or integrate new material. Plus by the time evening rolled around, invariably I was exhausted and wished I could just go home instead of running from my desk to a casino lounge to entertain people. Almost every night, I either couldn't get to sleep or I'd wake up with my to-do list racing through by head. You know shit's getting real when your stress level messes with your beauty sleep.

Then one morning in November 2017 during a meeting in a crowded Panera, the world around me started to spin. I pressed my palms into the table, looked at my client, and said, "I'm so sorry. I need to call my doctor." In the interest of full disclosure, I should tell you that while I don't consider myself to be a hypochondriac, I do have quite the talent for self-diagnosing minor ailments as worst-case scenarios. A headache is a brain tumor, an age spot is melanoma, and I don't know how many times I've attributed a twitch in my eye to Parkinson's.

Fortunately, my doctor said she could get me in immediately. My client offered to drive me there, but I insisted I was fine, despite the stroke I expected any moment. Turns out that neurotic inner voice was almost right. My blood pressure clocked in at an alarming 206/109, a "hypertensive crisis," which freaked me out even more. After I sufficiently calmed down, I was sent home with a prescription for high blood pressure medication. In retrospect, I'm surprised I wasn't rushed to the ER. My client called me later that afternoon to see how I was doing and admitted she had followed me to my doctor's office to make sure I got there okay. I so appreciated her concern and told her I might need an extra day to get her resume together. She responded with something like, "Um, yeah... don't worry about that."

After that episode, I tried like hell to manage my stress. I bought all kinds of herbal concoctions and CBD remedies from the dispensary down the street. I made half-hearted attempts at meditation, something I've yet to embrace although I often rattle off its benefits to others. I took baths in Epsom salts and lavender oil. Nothing seemed to do the trick. What I really needed was an "I Don't Give a Shit" pill because most of my stress was self-induced. My resumes had to be perfect—I've never been the "good enough" type—and I felt pressured to turn them over quickly despite the fact that most of my clients left their companies with months of severance pay and were in no big rush to get back into the daily grind. Just when I'd feel somewhat balanced, a company in town would have a big layoff and I'd be back in freak-out mode.

Fast forward a year and a half. I'm on vacation visiting my family in Albany, sitting in an Irish pub with my daughter and one of my best girlfriends. While they're talking and laughing, I'm thinking about my client list and what's going on in the office on the other side of the country. My heart starts pounding. *Seriously?* I'm stressed out on vacation with a Guinness in front of me and the most fun people on earth on either side of me? That moment was my tipping point.

I called my boss the next day and broke the news. He completely understood and wasn't surprised—he knew this day would come. I gave four months' notice, enough time to make sure my replacement would be thoroughly trained, all office documentation was up-to-date, and none of my clients would be left hanging. On Friday, July 19, 2019, my work gang threw me a wonderful send-off at my favorite Irish pub in Las Vegas. The next Monday morning it was all behind me.

Fortunately, my wakeup call happened at a pub on vacation and not in an emergency room, though it almost went down like that. So please, if your medicine cabinet is stocked with remedies for or an upset stomach or chronic headaches, if you can't remember when you last had a good night's sleep, if your blood pressure is inching up or periodically spikes into Stroke City like mine did, please get your act together and plan your exit now. At the risk of flaunting my flair for the dramatic, read this book and do the exercises as if your life depends on it.

You're the biggest kid in the sandbox. Whether you love or hate your job, you never want to be the smartest person at the conference table. You have no one to learn from, which is frustrating if you're a top performer who's eager to grow. Plus, you're often stuck doing all the heavy lifting, particularly if your co-workers have a sluggish work ethic and you can run circles around them. Think about your performance expectations—are they set so low that you barely have to make an effort? Hitting a home run is hardly a challenge if the left field wall is only thirty feet away. Staying too long in an uninspiring work environment can hurt you professionally. It's time to leave the kindergartners behind.

You work for an idiot and that person is not going anywhere. I'm going to repeat myself: The person you report to can make or break your happiness, and one of the most important aspects of your job is to make that person look good. You'll have zero motivation to do that if you have a tyrant of a boss who doesn't appreciate you or who passes off your deliverables as their own without giving credit where credit is due. If making that person look good means you're compromising your own integrity, or if you're answering to someone who's at all abusive or manipulative, you have to pack it up.

You're in a toxic work environment. Cliques, high turnover, rumor mills, narcissistic or authoritarian leadership, low morale… these are all signs of a dysfunctional culture. If you're in the Love Canal of the workplace and you're somehow able to disengage from the drama and negativity, hats off to you. Most of us don't have the fortitude to compartmentalize our lives like that. Better to seek out a more pleasant work environment than let that crap follow you home like dogshit on your shoe.

You're moody and ugly. Your difficult nature affects the people around you. Your kids walk on eggshells, your partner fights the urge to snuff you out in your sleep, and your friends are sick of listening to your "I hate work" tape. Soon everyone will avoid you and will be "busy" whenever you suggest getting together. Other people shouldn't have to be subjected to your piss-poor mood because you hate your job. Do something before you become a very lonely person.

The nature of your work goes against your core values. I've often told people the second worst day of my life was the day I accepted a job selling timeshares; the worst day was when I was fired for *not* selling timeshares. This was during the dark days after I moved to Las Vegas when I had zero, and I mean *zero*, money to live on.

I know some people like them, but money experts universally regard buying a timeshare as one of the worst financial decisions you can make. That was my belief as well, but you gotta do what you gotta do. They were willing to hire me, and I had no other job prospects on my radar.

And so there I was, giving presentations to tourists on the Las Vegas Strip who were clearly in front of me only for the free show tickets they'd receive in exchange for enduring my halfhearted sales pitch. They'd listen politely and laugh when I'd test some comedy material I was working on, and sometimes at the end I'd get a hug. One couple said being with me was the most fun they'd had in Vegas, which I thought was both sweet and terribly sad.

One morning I sat there positively hating myself as a young couple tried to rationalize a purchase that their current "robbing Peter to pay Paul" financial strategy clearly couldn't support. I finally interjected and said something that has never been uttered in the history of timeshare sales: "This may not be the best time for you to buy." They agreed and thanked me and gave me a hug. Later that day, the sales manager pulled me aside. I hadn't met the three-sale minimum during the first two weeks of employment, and well, per company policy he'd have to let me go.

That was not a shock. I had a feeling from the beginning that the only money I'd make in commission-based timeshare sales would be what I pulled in during the two-week paid training period. I didn't believe in the product and I couldn't bear to broker a deal that required people to make such a long-term financial commitment in a high-pressure, now-or-never sales structure.

I was soon able to secure another position, this time as a weight loss counselor with a now-defunct company that sold its own line of food products. I was grateful to have another two-week paid training period, during which I realized that although supporting people's weight loss goals was certainly aligned with my values, selling them crappy and overpriced food was not. On the last day of training, I told them this would not be for me.

That second false start spurred the most brilliant, and the most pathetic, idea that ever crossed my mind: What if I just kept accepting positions and then quit at the end of the paid training? That way I'd be making money while sitting in classes but would never have to do any actual work. Surely I could find a job somewhere with a nice, let's say, six-month paid training. Hell, maybe even a year. Think big, right?

As brainy as it was, I never followed through on that. Instead, I called a nice man I'd recently met at a spiritual lecture who owned a casino in a kind of scary part of town that tourists never visit. We met in a coffee shop near his house, and he offered me a job on the spot as his swing shift manager. Basically, all I had to do was sashay around the casino floor and be nice to people and dump ashtrays and empty beer bottles in the trash bins. Needless to say, that was not the best use of my fancy graduate school education, but I was not in a position to be picky. I was so very grateful to have an income. My gratitude was surpassed only by the sadness I felt for the folks sitting at the slot machines losing money when it looked like they hadn't sat in a dentist's chair in a very long time.

The lesson I learned is easy to recognize in hindsight: Yes, you do what you have to do, but it's always better if what you *have* to do is also aligned with your values. That "selling your soul for money" feeling contradicts the essence of what you're all about and erodes your self-esteem. You'll be happier somewhere else.

Your job simply doesn't bring you joy. That reason alone is good enough. Game over.

Bad reasons to stay in a job that you really should leave

You love your coworkers. If you leave, you'll miss them and they'll miss you. Oh, please. They aren't the only coworkers on earth that you'll ever get along with, and if you love them that much, you can socialize with them off the clock. I'm still close friends with people I worked with thirty years ago. Go find new kids to play with.

You're loyal to your boss or the company. I felt horrible when I told my boss that I was leaving. He was so good to me! But I was good to him, too. I made sure his Las Vegas operations ran smoothly and our clients received the highest quality outplacement services. My reputation and ability to cultivate relationships brought in a ton of new business. And you know what? The place didn't collapse after I left. No one is irreplaceable. So if it's in your best interest to pursue other opportunities, be thankful for the experience, but don't shortchange yourself by letting a sense of loyalty or obligation to your employer stand in your way.

Here's another way to look at this. If your boss got a memo from the corporate headquarters saying your position is hitting the bottom line the wrong way or that your whole department has become "redundant," despite your years of loyalty, I guarantee you'd still be out of a job. Be loyal to yourself and do what's in *your* best interest, not the company's.

Next year you'll get an extra week of vacation. Why on earth would that be a reason to stay? So you can have one more week away from a job you hate every day? No, just no.

You've been hoping for years that things will get better. As one of the characters on my beloved old soap opera once said, "Hope can be a virtue or a curse." If you're not seeing any real change after you've done everything you could to improve the situation, then tell me why you think things will change on their own.

You wonder whether you can learn something new. Sure, you know *this* job inside out, but how long will it take to pick up something new? And would you be any good at it? You can get so comfortable in a job that you start to lose confidence in your capabilities. Let that line of thinking go. You've already identified so many of your skills and talents, including five home run zones where you rock. Were you writing fiction when you did all that work in the personal branding chapter? I didn't think so.

You need to [fill in the blank] first. "I can't leave my job until my kids are out of college." "I need to lose 10 pounds before I can start interviewing." "I need to get my house in order before I can even think about my work life." Some reasons for staying where you are for now are valid; others are disguised procrastination. You know the difference. Don't kid yourself.

The money is too good to walk away from. Yes, I did say that if your financial obligations require the income you're currently bringing in and you don't think you'll see that kind of money if you make a move, then it's probably best to stay put. But if you've done salary research and find you can likely make that kind of money somewhere else, then what's holding you back?

You haven't had to look for a job in ages and don't know where to start. Stay with me. I'm going to take you through this soon.

You don't want to be a quitter. Who exactly is going to call you a quitter, and why would you care? Do *you* think it's smarter to stay in a lame situation than to peace out?

Let's say you moved from San Diego to New York City. You're not happy; it's busy and noisy and it's not what you thought it would be. Are you going to stay in New York and be miserable for the rest of your life? Just because you have years of experience doing something doesn't mean you have to continue to do it forever.

Singer-songwriter Bill Callahan has a line in one of his songs, "No matter how far wrong you've gone, you can always turn around." We've been told since childhood, "Don't be a quitter. Quitters always lose." But knowing when to leave a toxic situation, when to give up on something that's not working out, when to say good-bye and head in another direction... that's just being smart.

ॐ

There should never be one focal point that your entire universe revolves around, and that includes your job. Like a love partner, if you expect it to meet every one of your needs, you'll inevitably be disappointed. Keep your job in perspective. Maybe it isn't a destination, but the boat that takes you to where you really want to go. Maybe your workplace serves only to provide a structure that allows you to interact with cool coworkers you adore and the work itself is inconsequential.

Your job can totally suck and the rest of your life can be perfectly enjoyable as long as you have enough time and energy outside of work to enjoy real life. On the other hand, if you're wasting too much time watching mindless TV or scrolling though social media, you can't say you're serious about wanting more for yourself.

Nobody says you *have* to leave a job you hate. That's a personal choice. Just realize you're staying because you *want* to. Own that reality, don't complain about it. Don't make the people close to you miserable. It would be sad to stay in a job you hate, or not put forth any effort toward improving your work situation, just because you're too lazy or don't have the balls to make things happen.

Sorry, I think I lapsed into bossy voice. I warned you about that.

6. Your Financial Reality

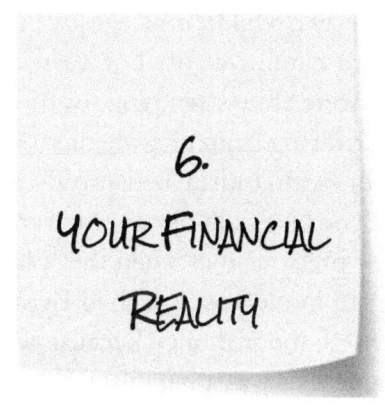

MONEY EQUALS FREEDOM, and the more stable your financial base is, the more options are available to you. For example, if you're leaning toward a major career change, chances are you won't be making the kind of money you're currently used to, at least not right out of the gate. Sure, you have the right educational background and years of experience in your current industry, and no doubt many of the skills you've honed over the years can transfer to a new direction. But you don't have years of experience in your new field of interest, and that can impact your immediate earnings. You don't want to head in a direction with substantially lower pay if it's not going to be enough to live on. Similarly, it would be impractical for you to decide to work part-time or to take a break from working to focus on creative pursuits if the bottom line doesn't work out.

Educate yourself about personal finance

If I were queen, money management would be a subject taught to every middle school and high school student instead of something stupid like trigonometry, which to this day I have never, *ever* used in real life. Somehow I've managed to get by without experiencing the practical application of a sine or cosine. Math is important when it comes to calculating thirty percent discounts on a cute pair of boots, but the fancy stuff beyond that is lost on me.

Personally, I didn't have any money to speak of until I was way into adulthood. When you have two children at age twenty-one, you start life in a financial hole that's hard to climb out of. For years the kids' dad and I lived paycheck to paycheck. We were always scraping for money, digging for change in the couch cushions and borrowing from piggy banks. Our home décor was a half-step above a college dorm, with Indian bedspreads and posters of rock stars thumbtacked to the walls. The kids didn't know we were broke—they thought we were cool—and it's kind of precious that when they played house, they'd pretend the Talking Heads front man in the poster, David Byrne, was their father. I felt I didn't need to educate myself about money because why learn about something you don't have? In hindsight, that was a big mistake.

Whatever your financial picture looks like, I urge you to do your research and learn as much as you can. Money management and personal finance is a huge area of study, and I know that navigating those waters can be overwhelming.

I'm a big fan of Lisa Chastain. Lisa is based in Las Vegas; I've heard her speak several times. Her bestselling book, *Girl, Get Your Shit Together,* is a no-nonsense guide that helps readers understand the psychological aspects of their relationship with money so they can make wise financial choices. Though her advice is targeted to female millennials, I found this book to be insightful and a good read for both women and men of any age.

Find a money management podcast that speaks to your financial situation. You're not ready to learn about investment strategies if you're working on getting out of debt. Listening regularly will motivate you to stay on track. It's okay if you don't quite understand everything at first. You'll get it eventually, and after a while you'll realize you're hearing things you've already learned. It's good to reinforce those concepts over and over.

Assess your current financial picture

In order to make any sound decisions about your future, you first need to have a solid understanding of what your financial picture looks like today. To put that picture into focus, you need to know how much money is coming in, how much is going out, and where it's going. If you haven't already, take the time to do the following:

- Make a list of all your monthly living expenses as well as any other expenses that might hit you once a year, such as auto registration fees and insurance premiums.
- Start tracking every cent you spend. Most people have a clear idea of their income, but not their spending. To create a spending plan, check out the free budgeting tools available online and see which one you find easiest to work with.
- If you haven't already, start to build a separate emergency fund of at least $1,000. Ideally, you want to have three to six months of living expenses on hand. Remember, it's called an *emergency* fund for a reason; this is money you don't touch unless you need a major car repair or if your water heater bursts. An amazing "today only" online sale is not an emergency. You'll be glad you did this. Having money on hand gives you peace of mind and allows you to address the unexpected spitballs life shoots your way.
- Know exactly what your debt looks like. Create a spreadsheet and list how much you owe, to whom, and the associated interest rates you pay. Based on your payment history, determine when you expect these debts to be paid in full.

Get out of debt ASAP

To have a truly happy and joyful life, you really need to get out of debt and stay out of debt. Once you've achieved that goal, I guarantee you'll never want that dark cloud hanging over you again.

If you're carrying debt, don't beat yourself up about it; you're certainly not alone. I know first-hand how that can happen. When I moved to Las Vegas, I had a terrible time finding a job even though I had a great looking resume and knew the ins and outs of how to conduct a job search. But I had no network here and since Vegas is a city of transients, employers seem wary of hiring people who've just landed here for fear they may soon decide to move back to where they came from. My savings dwindled with every passing month. I started using credit cards, not only to meet my basic living expenses, but also to buy things or take a trip I could no longer afford as a way to soothe my newly divorced broken heart. I rationalized my spending by telling myself, "You've been through a lot… you deserve this." It took me forever to learn that yes, you most certainly *do* deserve the best of everything, but that doesn't mean it's wise for you to buy it right now. The math has to work out, and if you buy things with money you don't have, you'll pay dearly for years to come.

I also understand how someone carrying a substantial amount of debt could think, "Hell, I'm in it this deep. What's another thirty bucks?" The thing is, when you increase your debt, you also increase your utilization ratio, which is the amount of credit you've used divided by the total credit you have available to you. When you reach certain levels of utilization, your credit score will drop. A low credit score can make life difficult in a number of ways; for example, some employers check a candidate's credit before extending an offer. Too much of a drop will prompt credit card companies to raise your interest rates, perhaps to astronomical levels, even if you've never been a day late on a payment. So the thirty bucks you charge at a restaurant because "you deserve to treat yourself" adds up, and it really does make a difference.

Treat getting out of debt as an emergency 9-1-1 situation. Becoming debt-free will require a one hundred percent commitment to making immediate changes in your lifestyle. It's a bare bones way of life that requires sacrifice. It won't be easy and it won't last forever, but it will be worth it. Sigmund Freud said, "A man with a toothache cannot fall in love." You cannot fully enjoy life when you're suffering with a huge financial toothache of debt.

So how do you get rid of it? The answer is similar to the eye-roll inducing "Exercise more, eat less" weight loss advice. In this case, it's "Make more, spend less." Annoying. Here are some best practices to help you get out of debt and maintain the debt-free lifestyle.

Use credit cards wisely, if at all. I have no problem charging things. In fact, I put almost everything on one credit card so I can rack up points for travel on Southwest Airlines. But I never carry a balance month to month, and when I charge something, I pay on my card right away to keep my balance at or near zero. Using credit cards requires discipline. If you don't feel you have that discipline, it's probably best for you to not use them at all. Pay for everything with cash or a debit card.

Understand that shopping is not a leisure activity. Shopping might be on the list of what brings you joy, but going to Marshall's to "look around" is an activity that needs to be put on hold. We all know there's no such thing as looking around without going home with something. Don't step into a store unless you're there to buy an item you truly need. That goes for online shopping, too. The only thing you shop for while you're chopping away your debt is food and other essentials.

Forget immediate gratification. Accept that you simply can't have everything you want right now. You can have them sometime, just not at this moment. I lose my freakin' mind when I hear people complaining about being broke and then I see them on social media showing off a new tattoo. The gratification that comes from paying for what you want in full will feel a million times better than charging it today.

Forget travel for now. Save for it. You're not going anywhere until you've paid off your debt, but I encourage you to plan every detail of your next vacation. Planning a vacation in itself is a joyful activity, and you'll be all set to go once you're ready. In the meantime, if you need to travel for a family emergency, that money comes out of your emergency fund. See? The key word is *emergency*.

Forget about eating out. Restaurants are out of the question, except *maybe* for a special occasion and only if you pay cash. Even then, find a deal. Mike and I know every happy hour special in town and unabashedly pull out that AARP card for ten percent discounts (and add the savings to the waitstaff's tip). We never go to expensive restaurants mainly because to me food is just future shit and flushing a fifty-dollar entrée down the toilet does not bring me joy. One year we celebrated Valentine's Day with the buck-fifty hotdog and soda special at Costco. We laughed our heads off at how goofy we are. Once you can afford fine dining, and if it brings you joy, certainly go for it. In the meantime, plan to eat at home.

Learn to say no. Get used to telling people, no, you can't get together for dinner. No, you're unable to attend their destination wedding. No, you're going to pass on that concert. And remember, "No" is a complete sentence. You don't owe anyone an explanation, but if you choose to share why you're declining, just say, "I'm working on some financial goals right now, and I'm being very careful to stick to my budget." Your true friends will respect your commitment. The funny thing is, you'll probably say no to a lot of stuff you really didn't want to do in the first place. This gives you a great excuse.

Let your kids hear you say no, too. It's okay to tell them you don't have the money saved for whatever they want right now. Don't say, "We can't afford it," say, "I don't have the money saved for that." They'll still love you, and if they don't, you have a real problem because you're raising little douches. My kids tell me all the time they're glad they didn't have everything handed to them, and they grew up to be lovely people.

While we're talking about kids, please don't push them to go to a college they can't afford. Their lives won't be ruined if they begin their academic career at a community college. It breaks my heart when I hear about young people starting out in a financial abyss because of student loan debt. Maybe *you* want them to live on campus and have a full college experience, but think twice before incurring such an obligation if both you and *they* haven't saved for it. That's right—have them work for it. High school kids can work, college kids can work. I want to throw up when parents say they don't want their kids to work so they can focus on their studies. Newsflash: they can do both. And they'll be more invested in their education if they, too, have to make some sacrifices.

Don't buy more car than you need. Know what you can realistically afford. The sales guy at the dealership will convince you that you can afford a $35,000 car because hey, it's only $375 a month for the next seven years and that works with your budget, right? No, you can afford to buy a $35,000 car if you can pay cash for it. Otherwise, you can afford only a monthly payment. There's a big difference. Unless you've saved enough to pay cash, consider opting for a less expensive pre-owned vehicle. Cars are made to last these days, as long as you keep them well maintained. You can find a reliable used Toyota or Honda that will serve you well for years.

Right now, both Mike and I own cars that are more than ten years old. I drive a 2009 Scion that I bought new for about $16,000. It's the size of a coffee table, but I don't need anything bigger, and it gets decent gas mileage. I hope I get another ten years out of it. It's super cute and it brings me joy, and I'm not out to impress anyone. Mike paid $10,000 for his 2007 Toyota Avalon in 2016. We charged it on my credit card, which gave me enough points on Southwest Airlines for a free trip, and I paid it off the day after the transaction posted.

If you have a car loan, pay it off as soon as you can and then continue to make monthly payments to yourself (in a separate account, if that makes sense to you). Then when you need a new vehicle, you'll have already saved for it.

Look for other opportunities to cut back. Review your spending. What can you live without? When did you last use your streaming subscriptions? Are you doling out money to adult kids who really should be paying for things on their own? Are you springing for ridiculous pony ride and bouncy house birthday parties for your kids because that's what other parents are doing? Climbing out of debt means saying no to your ego. Learn how to do your own nails. Clean the house and do the landscaping yourself. Use the self-service car wash. Throw the money you've saved toward your debt.

Look for opportunities to bring in more money. Chances are you're going to make the most money doing what you already do; that's where your education, expertise and experience lie. Even if continuing down this path is not exactly bringing you joy, your immediate goal is to get out of debt, and that *will* bring you joy. It's probably best to stay in this line of work for now and figure out how you can make more money doing it. Are there advancement opportunities at the company you work for? Do you see an unmet need that your talents can fulfill, and that would justify a higher salary? Can you make a case for a salary increase based on your current responsibilities? Should you make a move to another company that pays better?

You know where your talents lie—what can you do as a side hustle? What can you sell? Go through your garage and closets and weed out what doesn't bring you joy. Turn crap into cash. Make adult kids living under your roof pay rent. I understand you want to help them out, but isn't it time they learn responsibility? You're not doing them a favor by prolonging their adolescence. Do whatever you can to bring in more money and reduce your debt.

Hold yourself accountable. Share your debt-free goal with a person you trust and create a schedule to update that person on your progress. We tend to do better when we know someone is watching.

Be aware of the pitfalls of borrowing. You may be tempted to borrow money from a family member or a close friend to pay off your debt. Don't. For one, you'll deny yourself the satisfaction of having accomplished it on your own. What's more important is that when you borrow money from someone you know, you're giving that person an unspoken power over you, and like it or not, it's only natural for them to start scrutinizing your spending. They'll wonder how you can afford so many trips to Starbucks, without knowing somebody gave you a gift card. If you do borrow money, draw up a written contract for paying it back. In that case, everything should be cool as long as you honor the terms you've agreed upon. Try not to do this, though. A real change in behavior can occur only over time. It's better for you to develop new habits and a new mindset. Otherwise, you risk falling back into the same mess.

Stop paying "stupid tax." We've all done dumb stuff that ends up costing us money, usually due to procrastination or simply not being on top of things. Subscriptions and introductory offers you forgot to cancel, returns that you didn't bring back on time, any type of late fees, food in your refrigerator that goes bad, postage for express delivery because you waited too long… these are all examples of stupid tax. Whether you're in debt or not, track your stupid tax and vow to reduce it.

※

Your current financial situation determines the options available to you in your work life, but you may not be the only person who should have a say in your life decisions. Before you start following your dreams, make sure you're not setting your family up for a nightmare. A change in your career can also change the family dynamics. Taking on a side hustle will result in less time to spend with the kids. Being obligated to a new pursuit may mean your partner will have to pick up the slack. Think about how your intentions could affect the people you love.

7. Explore the Possibilities

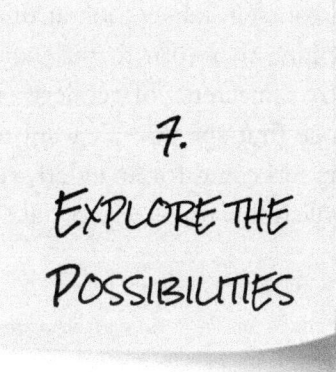

LET'S RECAP THE SELF-ASSESSMENT WORK you've done so far. At this point, you've identified the following:

- What brings you joy
- Your personal brand (and you've written a personal branding statement that encapsulates who you are and what you have to offer)
- Five areas where you knock it out of the park (your strongest talents)
- What makes you different (where your superpower lies)
- Your life's mission (or at least you're thinking about it)
- Your optimal work conditions
- If you're currently working, whether you want to stay where you are or move on to something different
- What your financial picture looks like
- Other factors that could play into your future

Now that you've collected all this information, let's figure out what you're going to do with it. What's the best outlet for your talents? Who can benefit from what you have to offer? What type of work would bring you joy?

Exercise: Identify Preliminary Possibilities

Before you do this exercise yourself, take a look at this completed example done by a stay-at-home mom looking to return to the workforce. To give you some background, she has two semesters of college in elementary education, considerable office experience (but she doesn't want to work in an office again), and for the past several years has cared for an elderly relative who recently passed away. I deliberately didn't polish this up so you could see it as it was written.

Example: Identify Preliminary Possibilities	
Skills, Knowledge, Experience	**Interests, Personality Traits, Values**
Music – local singer-songwriter (folk), back-up singer in regional reggae band	Artistic sense of style in clothing, jewelry, and home decor
Plays guitar	Fitness – dancing, walking, hiking, exercise videos
Decorative painting – furniture, trinkets	Party decorations on a budget—knows how to work the dollar store
Dancing – years of experience teaching creative movement to children	Loving, happy, cares for others
Good writing skills and command of grammar	Friendly, funny, spirited
Elder companion (does not want to do direct care)	Makes humorous YouTube videos
	Likes babies, old people, children
Limited Microsoft Word, Internet, social media (does not love technology)	Investigating – *Dateline* and murder mystery junkie
Makes amazing Halloween costumes	Organic cooking
Organizing living spaces	
Assembling things	
Driving	
Research	

Possibilities to Explore

1. Activities director in assisted living facility
2. Teacher's aide – daycare, preschool, elementary school
3. Work at funky grocery store or food co-op
4. Organize and decorate kids' bedrooms
5. Secret shopper
6. Create and sell humorous t-shirts
7. Senior companion
8. Turn YouTube videos into a business
9. Expand reach as singer-songwriter -- Sing at weddings, funerals, private parties
10. Decorate and entertain at children's parties – music, art projects

Do Want You Want

Now it's your turn. Since you've already done the work in the previous chapters, the top half of this next exercise won't be hard. In the column on the left, list what you're good at and what you know about. It's okay if it's not job related or if you've never been paid for doing it. In the right column, list your interests, your personality traits, and your values. Don't try too hard to categorize everything into the appropriate columns—just get it out of your brain and onto the page.

Once you do that, try to come up with ten possible avenues to explore. These could be full-time or part-time jobs, after-hours side hustles, personal hobby-type pursuits, volunteer activities—that's up to you. Focus on what you imagine you would enjoy doing. What gets you jazzed just thinking about it? Right now, you're just brainstorming, so don't censor yourself or overthink this. Jot down ideas as they come to you.

Chapter 7. Explore the Possibilities

Identify Preliminary Possibilities	
Skills, Knowledge, Experience	**Interests, Personality Traits, Values**

Possibilities to Explore

1.
2.
3.
4.
5.
6.
7.
8.
9.
10.

You might ask someone who knows you well to help with this. Sometimes your strengths are more apparent to other people than they are to you, and an outsider looking in may suggest possibilities that haven't crossed your mind. A word of caution, though: Consider what others have to say, but don't let anyone talk you out of something that excites you before you've given yourself a chance to research and explore what it's all about. If a friend says, "I know someone who did that kind of work and she hated it" or "My neighbor did that and he said the money was terrible," take that information with a grain of salt. Keep in mind that people sometimes project their own fears onto your situation. A possibility you're considering could be met with, "I don't know, that sounds awfully risky…" if they themselves are afraid to try something new. Some people may be so insecure with their own self-worth or be so ego-driven that they secretly may not want you to succeed. That's pretty sad, but it's possible.

Even people who truly mean well sometimes they have no clue what they're talking about. Or they may have a thought process that's just plain weird. I'm reminded of women my age who say they don't want to start dating again because "they don't want to have to take care of anybody." *What?* Would it be impossible to find someone who's healthy or to keep the relationship on the casual side? Before they've even met anyone, they're projecting they're going to be together long enough for the guy's health to go south, *and* to the point where he'll need a caregiver. Do you see how crazy that is? Don't let someone's kooky line of thinking put the kibosh on what might, in fact, work out well for you.

Dig deeper and do a gap analysis

If you're not sure what types of jobs exist for someone with your talents and/or what the qualifications for those jobs are, go to any job board and type one of your strongest skills in the search field. Leave the geographic location blank. Right now, you're not searching for a particular opportunity near where you live, you just want to see what jobs exist on earth that match your skill set. For example, if you type "strong research skills" or just "research" in the search box, you'll see a million different jobs all over the country in a thousand different industries. You won't be interested in most of them, but some will catch your eye. Those are the ones you want to look further into. Another way to uncover possibilities is to simply Google "jobs that require research skills." Have fun with this. Add jobs that grab your attention to your list of possibilities to explore.

Review your list and identify the possibilities that appeal to you the most. Moving forward, you'll want to research what each one realistically involves and how it could fit into your life right now. For the employment options that catch your eye, look for the following:

- Both the essential and "nice to have" qualifications for that type of position
- Educational requirements
- Typical responsibilities
- Average earnings

Find a few job postings in your targeted location for each of the possibilities you're most excited about. Copy and paste the links into a spreadsheet for future reference. Don't worry if you don't meet every single requirement. That's not necessarily a deal breaker; job posts are often written for an ideal candidate who may or may not exist. If you think you would be more marketable by adding new skills to your repertoire or by further developing the skill set you already have, then make a plan for how that's going to happen. Fortunately, you can learn almost anything online, and a lot of it for free. Google "free online courses" and your area of interest and see what you come up with.

If you're thinking of pursuing self-employment, either as your primary source of income or as a side hustle, you'll want to research:

- The best legal structure for your business
- Required licenses and permits
- Insurance you may need
- Self-employment taxes
- How to write a business plan (which includes your marketing and sales strategy)

Try not to feel overwhelmed by any of this. Just because you don't know something right now doesn't mean you can't learn about it. Dogen, the great Zen master, said, "When you walk in the mist, you get wet." So start walking in the mist. Start researching whatever it is you need to find out. This couldn't be easier;

it's not like you have to scour the Help Wanted section in the newspaper or navigate the Dewey Decimal system at the public library like in the olden days. The world is literally at your fingertips!

Also think about who in your network of contacts can help you. Review the list of people in your tribe. Who is already doing, or has done, what you'd like to do? Who would be happy to share their knowledge and point you in the right direction? In an upcoming chapter I'll show you how to reach out to them, but in the meantime, make a list of everyone you want to contact.

Are you willing to pay your dues?

As you learn more about a direction you're considering, you may come to realize it's not anything you really want to do after all. For example, let's say you love plants and gardening. Every time you have a crappy day at work you think about doing something with gardening and wonder why you haven't looked into it yet. Finally, you Google "jobs for people who love to garden" and you see a variety of options including landscape architect, horticulturist, ornamental horticulturist, plant pathologist, florist, nursery worker, self-employed gardener, and more.

After you look further into these possibilities, a few realizations come to light. 1) You don't want to go back to school to study horticulture or landscape architecture or anything else, 2) A job in a florist shop or nursery wouldn't pay enough to live comfortably and you'd probably have to work weekends, which you don't want to do, and 3) Starting your own landscaping or gardening business would require you to learn all that self-employment stuff and writing a business plan seems like a lot of work and you would probably need a website and you don't feel like learning about that, either. (Although you totally could if you wanted to.)

This is when I would diplomatically suggest that since you're not willing to pay your dues, you should give up that dream. Just understand that you're giving it up only because you don't want it enough to work and sacrifice for it. That's fine. Letting go of a dream can be liberating. You're no longer holding on to an unfulfilled fantasy and all the angst and guilt that comes with it. You no longer have to say, "Oh, I always wanted to..." because now you know you really don't want that at all. So find something you *do* want and that you're willing to work toward.

I understood from the beginning that I was not going to pursue comedy as a means of generating any significant source of income. First and foremost, I didn't want to give up the money I was finally pulling in from my day job, especially since my priority was to pay off debt. And as much as I love to travel, the thought of driving for hours to gigs for the kind of money I'd be making and staying in crappy motels or sharing a "comedy condo" of questionable housekeeping standards with people I don't know is just not me. Even securing local gigs requires a lot of hanging around the clubs to get in face time with the bookers and to network with other comics. Since I had to work in the morning, I didn't do that as much as I would have liked, either.

The bottom line is, I can't bemoan the fact that I don't have a brilliant career in comedy. If for no other reason—like, say, having the talent—I wasn't willing to pay my dues. I have great respect for people who dream big and reach for the stars, but I wasn't willing to suffer for my art. Not that much, anyway. So for me, comedy is a side hustle. Some career comedians would call me a "hobby comic," perhaps with a bit of discountenance. I'm cool with that. I admire them for what they had to do to get where they are, but I chose a different path.

If you're seriously leaning toward pursuing creative endeavors or making a major career change, plan on paying some dues. Your new position may not have the status of your current title; in fact, you may have to start toward the bottom of the pyramid. You may not make as much money. You may have to invest some time and money into gaining a new skill set. You may have to work a schedule that wouldn't be your preference. You may have to take direction from people, instead of the other way around. You're not going to be the top dog. Make sure your ego can handle such a move.

You don't have to jump into the deep end right away; you can dip your toe in the water and see how it feels. Take on a short-term contract gig in your new area of interest. If you want to explore a career in teaching, try substituting for a while. I'm a huge proponent of doing volunteer work. You'll feel appreciated, you'll gain experience, and you'll probably expand your network with some valuable connections.

DO WANT YOU WANT

Exercise: Identify Action Items

List the five options you came up with in the Identifying Preliminary Possibilities exercise that appeal to you the most and then list the steps to take to transform this possibility to reality. What requires further research? Who do you need to talk to? What can you do to acquire that knowledge? Be as specific as possible.

Once you've done this exercise, you'll know what to do. Commit to getting these things done.

Action Items for Each Option
Option #1:
Action items: • • • •
Option #2:
Action items: • • • •
Option #3:
Action items: • • • •

Option #4:

Action items:

-
-
-
-

Option #5:

Action items:

-
-
-
-

8. Assemble the Package

BY NOW YOU'VE DONE A TON OF HARD WORK, unless you skipped over all the exercises with a promise to get back to them later. In that case, march your ass back to Chapter 3 and get to work on them now. If you're one of the good people who followed instructions, you're ready to package up what you have so far. In this chapter, you'll learn how to present your talents and experience in a resume and on social media, particularly LinkedIn. I know this isn't the most fun chapter to read, but imagine how I felt having to write it.

Write a kick-ass resume

I can't overstate the importance of taking the time to create the best resume possible. A strong resume loaded with quantified accomplishments can open doors and result in more lucrative job offers. That means more money coming your way, and money equals freedom and freedom equals joy. Excuse my flair for the dramatic, but a kick-ass resume can change your life.

Writing your own resume can be maddening. I wish I could give you a formula, as I did with your branding statement, but resumes are much more complex. Part of the problem is there's not one way to go about it. That's because your resume's content and where that information is positioned on the page depends on many different factors, most of which are driven by your objective and how your skills, talents, and experience support that objective.

To confuse things more, if you show your resume to ten different people, you'll get ten different opinions about how it "should" look. You'll hear things like, "You need a slick format to make your resume stand out," "Education always goes at the end," and "People won't read anything longer than a one-page resume." This may cause you to second-guess your approach, and you can't go changing your resume to accommodate every bit of feedback. You'll drive yourself nuts and that's simply not the best use of your time.

As in life, you'll never be able to please everybody, so give up that dream. I'm not saying other people's opinions don't matter; they do. By all means, run your resume by colleagues who know your work and your targeted industry. They may offer a perspective you haven't thought of. And I would certainly be concerned if nobody seems to understand a particular bullet on your resume—that means you need to reword it.

Here is the approach I take, and along the way I'll share my rationale. It's hard for me to give you proper guidance because I can think of an exception to almost everything I say. I often break my own rules because so much depends on the individual situation. The bright side of this torturous task is there's no such thing as a perfect resume; it only has to be good enough. And you've already done the hardest part: figuring out your objective, or what you want to do.

Contact information

All you need here is your name, phone number, and email address. Don't bother with your street address—no one will be sending you snail mail—but it doesn't hurt to add your city, state, and zip code. I would definitely include that information if you've recently relocated to the area where you're conducting your search.

Nothing screams "I'm not keeping up with the times!" louder than an AOL, Yahoo, or Hotmail email address. I know they still work perfectly, but they're perceived as being old school. Get yourself a Gmail account at least for the job search. Make sure your email's username doesn't reveal anything it shouldn't, such as your year of birth ("DebbieD1974") or your love of the party life. I once had to advise a client that "Vegaswino" probably wasn't the best choice.

Once it's ready for prime time, include a link to your LinkedIn profile. We'll talk about that soon.

Introduction

At first pass, readers typically spend less than ten seconds on a resume. However, they will continue to read through, or at least scan, your resume more carefully if you grab their attention up front. Keep in mind people read from top to bottom and they understand from general to specific. Therefore, the most important part of any document is the top third of the first page—this is where you engage your reader. The content you select to place here sets the stage for what's to come and gives the reader a context in which to put the details that follow.

Resume title. I generally advise against generic headings such as "Professional Overview" or "Summary of Qualifications." Titles such as "Senior Human Resources Leader" or "Office Manager / Executive Assistant" or "Retail Operations Manager" are much more descriptive. The title of your resume will probably match the "what you are" segment of your branding statement. If you want, you can add a subtitle underneath.

Titling your resume succinctly communicates your objective, and that's why you don't need a heading that says, "Objective." Generally, what's under that is junk and says absolutely nothing: *To secure a challenging position that uses my strengths and abilities.... blah, blah.* Rubbish! Why would you waste the precious real estate at the top of the page with that?

Furthermore, an objective tells the reader what you're looking for, which means it focuses on *your* needs. The rule for any type of business writing is to focus on meeting the needs of the reader. Always make your writing *reader*-focused, not *writer*-focused. A prospective employer reads a resume thinking, "What's in this for me?"

Introductory paragraph or bullets. This is where you communicate the best you have to offer. What *must* a potential employer know about you? Don't get too specific; the reader does not yet have a context in which to put any details. You can present this information in the form of a paragraph (no more than a few lines) or a few bullets. I'm a fan of bullets—they help lead readers through your text.

Areas of expertise and technical skills. If you have a broad and diverse background, you'll probably have some additional content here. Listing your areas of expertise loads your resume with keywords that will enhance your chances of getting through the automated resume screening tools that some companies use to streamline their hiring process.

Here are a couple of examples to give you an idea of what this top section can look like using this approach.

Sample Resume Introduction

OFFICE OPERATIONS MANAGER

- Collaborative, motivated, and integrity-driven team player with 20+ years of experience managing front and back-office operations in diverse industries
- Possess diplomatic interpersonal skills and an enthusiastic approach to building relationships with clients and colleagues
- Demonstrate a superior command of grammar, usage, and style in written communication
- Effectively organize and prioritize workflow; easily adapt to changing priorities and challenging situations
- Consistently exceed business and customer service goals

Areas of expertise:

− Resource management	− Building security and access
− Scheduling	− Accounts payable / accounts receivable
− Record management	− Payroll
− Budgeting	− System customization

Technical skills: Microsoft Office and various accounting, HR, and CRM systems

Note the subtitle in this example:

Sample Resume Introduction

Sales and Marketing Executive – Industrial Supply

Business Development ♦ Relationship Management ♦ Team Leadership

- Results-focused professional with extensive experience leading sales and marketing operations to achieve strong and sustainable revenue growth as well as market enhancement

- Possess a passion for cultivating and managing relationships with top-tier decision makers and external business partners; effectively integrate "Voice of the Customer" into sales and marketing programs, generating richer results

- Have held integral roles in acquisition initiatives to achieve growth goals and align critical business functions including sales / marketing due diligence and post-acquisition integration

- Well-versed in Lean and Kaizen principles and practices to improve process efficiency

- A respected leader and solution provider who enjoys developing high-performing cross-functional and geographically dispersed teams

Additional areas of expertise:

– Product management	– New product launch
– Key account management	– Distributor management
– Competitive analysis	– Profit and loss (P&L) management

Do Want You Want

Remember the example from the "Identify Preliminary Possibilities" exercise in the last chapter? This is how that stay-at-home mom's information translated to the top part of her resume:

Sample Resume Introduction

COMPASSIONATE, SERVICE-ORIENTED PROFESSIONAL

- More than 10 years of experience in diverse environments, including 8 years managing school operations and teaching creative movement to children
- Excellent interpersonal and writing abilities; exceptional organizational skills
- Possess a friendly and outgoing personality, keen sense of humor, and professional appearance
- Proven ability to work under stress without compromising accuracy
- Enjoy creative pursuits as local singer-songwriter and backup vocalist

Computer skills: Microsoft Word, Excel, Zoom, Google Meet, social media

---

Here's an example where the resume title reinforces what the candidate is seeking.

Sample Resume Introduction

BUSINESS STUDENT SEEKING INTERNSHIP OPPORTUNITY

- Ambitious, results-focused professional with an entrepreneurial spirit and a collaborative leadership style rooted in building trust and cultivating relationships
- Possess congenial interpersonal skills and an ability to write succinct marketing content
- Enjoy travel and appreciate diversity; easily adapt to cultural differences in communications

Technical skills: Microsoft Office, Google Workspace, Squarespace web design, social media platforms

Sometimes people ask whether they need different versions of their resume to match the position they're applying for. By structuring your introduction using this approach, you can easily target your resume to any particular opportunity with a few minor tweaks. Usually, you can simply replace some bullets with the requirements listed on the job posting. When doing this, try to use some of the exact phrasing as in the posting or match it as closely as possible.

Experience

Position overview. Typically, you start with your most recent experience and then work your way back in reverse chronological order. Under each title you've held, write a short sentence or two that provides a broad overview of the position's responsibilities. Again, you do this because people understand from general to specific and you want to give your reader a context in which to interpret the details that are to follow.

Sample Position Overviews
UNIVERSITY NAME, City, State   (2017 – 2019) **Assistant to the Dean,** School of Art Handled highly sensitive and confidential information including faculty contracts and performance evaluations, financial records, promotion and tenure review cases, and sabbatical applications.
COMPANY NAME, City, State   (2019 – Present) **IT Technical Writer** Edit a variety of technical documents including system specifications, procedures, and user interface guides for this regional not-for-profit health plan. (Contract position through ABC Consulting.)
COMPANY NAME, City, State   (2015 – Present) **Senior Consultant,** Program Management Managed the end-to-end process for customization and vendor deployments of cyber security tools for clients in technology services and digital transformation.

Quantified accomplishments. From there, add a few bullet points of accomplishments, preferably showing measurable results. Most of the resumes that have come my way look like job descriptions converted into resume format with the person's education slapped at the end. DON'T DO THAT! Job descriptions are full of tasks and responsibilities, and usually reflect the minimal expectations of the position. You're better than that. Your goal is not to show *what* you do, but to show you're *good* at what you do.

Coming up with these accomplishments can be a pain in the ass, but good news: I have a formula. We can call this the CAB approach, which stands for Circumstance, Action, and Benefit.

The CAB approach to writing accomplishments

Circumstance: Think of a circumstance at work that needed to be changed. Maybe a process was broken, money or time was being wasted, or a need wasn't being met. Something was off.

Action: What action did you take to correct the circumstance or meet that need? How did you improve a process? What solution did you implement (or suggest)?

Benefit: What benefit resulted from your action? Plug in figures whenever you can. How much time or money was saved? By how much did your solution increase efficiency or productivity?

Write up as many of these CAB stories as you can think of. They don't have to be perfectly articulated; a stream of consciousness is fine. Just get your thoughts down. You may feel some CABs aren't significant enough to include on your resume but hang on to them anyway. They'll come in handy when we get to interviewing.

Next, translate these stories into a single sentence or two that focuses on the action you took and the resulting benefit. Begin this sentence with an action verb. Use present tense if it's something that's still ongoing, past tense if it happened in the past. This example shows a CAB story translated into an accomplishment statement that can now be plugged into the resume.

CHAPTER 8. ASSEMBLE THE PACKAGE

Sample accomplishment using the CAB approach

Circumstance: The company's website needed to be transformed to a full e-commerce site. This was a huge $20 million project.

Action: I performed requirements analysis and testing of the new site.

Benefit: Customer experience was improved, and revenue increased by 17%.

Accomplishment statement:
- Performed requirements analysis and testing during the $20M transformation of the company's website to a full e-commerce site. Efforts enhanced functionality, improved customer experience, and resulted in a 17% increase in revenue.

You would never find that accomplishment statement on a job description. No, the job description would probably say something like, "Analyze business requirements and test functionality of new software." The quantified accomplishment statement is so much stronger, right?

Do Want You Want

Here's another example:

Sample accomplishment using the CAB approach
Circumstance: Out-of-state clients were being serviced by their local affiliates, who did not always meet our quality standards or provide the same deliverables. ***Action:*** I created a process that enabled us to deliver services remotely. ***Benefit:*** We were able to retain up to $25K in monthly revenue that was previously being referred out. All clients received the same services and we had better control over the quality. ***Accomplishment statement:*** • Implemented a process to serve out-of-state clients remotely instead of referring to local third-party affiliates. Efforts ensured consistent quality of service delivery and increased monthly revenue by $25K.

Accomplishment statements can't possibly tell the entire story, just enough to get your point across. Ideally, you'll have the chance to explain in further detail during an interview.

Sometimes this CAB approach doesn't exactly work for what you have to say. That's okay. Try to present yourself in the strongest way possible, plugging in figures wherever you can. The following examples show how much stronger your content is when it's quantified. Again, nothing in the "Strong" column would be found on a job description.

| The Strength of Quantified Accomplishments ||
Weak	Strong
Manage all aspects of annual event planning and production.	Manage annual event planning and production, from concept to execution, for 2,500+ attendees.
Responsible for budget management.	Manage a program budget of $30K.
Provide HR leadership both domestically and abroad.	Provide global HR leadership for 3,400 employees in 53 countries.
Produce the vast majority of the division's total monthly sales volume.	Produce more than 80% of the division's total monthly sales volume.
Consistently delivered projects on time and with minimal revenue loss.	Achieved 99% on-time delivery with <5% revenue loss per project.

Loading your experience section with quantified accomplishments gives you the edge over your competitors who simply converted their job description into something that looks like a resume. Here are some other recommendations for this section:

- Generally, employers are most interested in what you've been doing the past five to ten years. Beyond that, just hit the highlights or reference previous experience with a line such as, "Prior to 2015, held progressively responsible positions in retail management."
- Avoid redundancies. If you did basically the same thing in several different positions, don't bother going into those details again and again. This is another reason to focus on your CAB accomplishments—they will be different for each job, even if the responsibilities of those positions were similar. Think of a resume not as a documentation of what you did every year of your work life, but as a presentation of what you can do for a prospective employer—how you can meet their needs and solve their problems—with your quantified accomplishments serving as proof of your ability to get those things done.

- Allocate the space on your resume according to how strongly the experience supports your objective.
  - If you intend to advance in the path you're on, you'll probably devote more space to your current job and less to each position as you go back in time.
  - If you'd like to return to the type of work you did years ago, provide more details about that experience. Again, because people read from top to bottom, I would offer that experience first, under the heading "Related Experience." Then present your unrelated experience in reverse chronological order under an "Additional Experience" heading.
- Avoid putting anything on your resume that you never want to do again, even if you do it well. Your reader assumes you're happy to perform whatever they see on there. If you need to include that type of experience to account for time, don't devote a lot of space to it on the page and certainly don't highlight it in the introductory section of your resume.
- If you're changing careers or want to downshift into a less demanding role, the details of your experience might not be as relevant as they would be if you were to continue in that line of work. Pick and choose the accomplishments that would be most applicable to your objective.
- Place awards and other recognitions as the last bullet under the position you held when you received them.
- Unless you need to account for time, omit a side hustle such as a consulting practice. A prospective employer could wonder whether you're fully committed to working for them or if you'll just be marking time until your own business takes off. In truth, that may be the case, but no one needs to know.

- If you want to talk about something during an interview, make sure it's on your resume. Unless you're interviewing with a psychic, how will anyone know to ask you about it? I've worked with clients who said they didn't want to give away "the whole story" in their resume so they would have something to talk about in the interview. That's not how it works. A resume is not a mystery novel; you won't spoil the ending.

About functional resumes. You may be familiar with functional resumes. With this type of resume, your experience and accomplishments are categorized according to your areas of ability, followed by your employment history. I rarely feel this is the best approach because no one can tell which positions you were in when those accomplishments happened. Recruiters and hiring managers like to have a time and place perspective, and with a functional resume that is lost. By expecting your reader to piece together your career story, you're making more work for them, and that's something you never want to do in any type of business communication.

Education and training

The heading "Education and Training" is fine, but I prefer "Professional Development" because you can stick so much under that—your education, company-provided training, certifications, and anything else related to your professional growth such as conference presentations, publications, and affiliations. If you're just starting your career and don't have any additional training or affiliations, simply use the heading "Education."

DO WANT YOU WANT

Sample Education and Training Section

PROFESSIONAL DEVELOPMENT

B.S., Chemical Engineering, RENSSELAER POLYTECHNIC INSTITUTE, Troy, NY
Professional Engineer (P.E.) Licensure, State of New York certification, 2020

Plant safety training:

- Process Hazard Analysis
- Chemical Process Safety
- OSHA 511
- Budgeting
- Hazard Identification & Risk Assessment
- Combustible Dust Hazard Recognition
- Hazard and Operability Study
- System Customization

Community leadership:

- Advisory committee member, State University of New York, Community Public Service program; 2017 – Present
- Commissioner, Central Creek Volunteer Fire Department: 2014 - Present

---

- If you didn't finish your degree, you can still list the school, city, and state and then on the next line say something like, "Completed 86 credits toward B.A. in Economics" or "B.A., Economics in progress." If you took only a couple of courses say, "Completed coursework in Economics." The point is, if you have any college at all, make it known even if you barely dipped your toe in the higher education water. I think it's fine to list any free online courses you've completed as long as they required substantial effort and support your objective.

- I generally don't include the year of graduation unless coursework was completed within the past few years. That said, if a "more mature" client finished a degree ten years ago, I'll put that date on there to reinforce that the person is a lifelong learner.

- Include only the company-provided training that is relevant to your skill set and that you've taken in the past couple of years. No need to list standard HR training everyone in the company has to take such as sexual harassment or workplace diversity training.

- List only current or very recent professional and community affiliations. Don't include political, religious, or ethnic affiliations unless you are absolutely sure that mentioning them will increase the likelihood of your being considered.
- If you're a recent college graduate, I would place your education after your introductory bullets since your degree is hot off the press and your experience is probably limited to an internship and summer jobs.

Sample Recent College Graduate Introduction

INFORMATION TECHNOLOGY PROFESSIONAL – ENTRY LEVEL

- Adaptable, outgoing, and energetic recent graduate seeking position as Business Analyst, Technical Sales Representative, or IT Support Specialist
- Tenacious troubleshooting abilities and diplomatic communication skills; effectively relay technical information to non-technical audiences
- Committed to providing the highest level of service to both internal and external customers
- Possess a solid understanding of computer hardware structure; able to assemble a PC from components

Technical skills: HTML, SQL, Bootstrap front-end web development framework, various development environments, Microsoft Office

EDUCATION

B.S., Information Technology, 2021
STATE UNIVERSITY OF NEW YORK, Plattsburgh, NY

Relevant coursework:

- Software Engineering
- Computer Security
- Project Management
- Information Systems Analysis and Design
- Database and Web Applications
- System Architecture

Other possible headings

I think it's a good idea to include other aspects of your background that you'd like a prospective employer to know about, such as experience you've gained through an avocation or volunteer work that provides insight into your character. In that case, you might use the heading "Professional and Personal Development" or use separate headings or subheadings such as "Volunteer Service" or "Additional Experience."

Sometimes an interviewer would ask about my hospice volunteer experience (and probably think I'm a much nicer person than I actually am), and I'm certain I landed two tech writing gigs by including stand-up comedy on my resume. I had one interview where that's all the guy wanted to talk about, and by the end of the day I was hired. Thankfully, he wasn't one of those "say something funny" people who expects comedians to be entertaining 24/7. No, he was a wannabe comic who interpreted my polite smiles as validation of his wittiness. Almost daily, he'd lay his cringeworthy new bits on me, inevitably concluding, "You can use that," with an index finger pointing in the air. When his uncle died of a stroke, I fully expected him to quip, "Guess it wasn't a stroke of luck!" He didn't, though, and now I have to live with the fact that my brain created that line, not his.

Anyway, put whatever you want in these last sections as long as it's nothing weird and is fairly recent. I once had a client in his late fifties who insisted on keeping his Eagle Scout designation on his resume. I respect the achievement, but dude, that's an old glory. Another client, who looked like he'd go into cardiac arrest trudging to the refrigerator, was still crowing about his college football days. I get that—it pained me when it was time to take my hospice experience off my resume. I enjoyed having readers infer that I'm a lovely and patient person. Now I'll have to find some other way to contribute to the karma bank, you know, to make up for all the drinking and swearing.

Layout and page length

You may be tempted to wow your reader with flashy, graphics-based layouts. I'm not a fan. The templates I've seen are quite restrictive, and though they might be okay for someone who doesn't yet have a lot of content for their resume, they don't seem to serve more experienced candidates. I know you want your resume to stand out, and it will if it's loaded with quantified accomplishments that show you're good at what you do. Content is king (or queen), not graphics. That said, the visual appeal of your resume is very important. Although initially it's read on the screen, no doubt your resume will be printed out before the interview. Make sure it has enough white space to allow for the interviewer's handwritten notes.

The length of your resume is driven by your objective and how extensive your background is. I cringe when clients cram twenty years of experience onto a single page using a four-point font. I told one guy, "Yes, you achieved your goal of having a one-page resume. Unfortunately, it's unreadable." Maybe people recall hearing the one-page rule from their college's career services department, which would make sense since new graduates generally don't have the experience to fill two pages. There's nothing wrong with a two-page resume, or even three or four pages if that's what it takes to tell your story and present your background in the context of your objective.

What to look for in a professional resume writer

If all this is making you bonkers, consider hiring a professional. That will cost you—plan on spending a few hundred dollars—but think of it as an investment in your future. Having a professionally written resume can make a huge difference in the types of jobs you're considered for and the salary being offered. You want to start a new position at the highest salary possible because that figure serves as the baseline for your future earnings.

Anyone can call themselves a professional resume writer and if you don't know better, you could pay good money for something mediocre. Have a good sense of the person you're trusting to make you look brilliant. Before you hand over a dime, check out the following:

Their background. The person doesn't need to have a degree in English or technical writing, but solid writing skills and an eye for layout are paramount. Someone with an understanding of career development and years of experience writing resumes for clients in many different industries, or at least in your industry, would be ideal.

Their approach. Competent resume writers will ask you a million annoying questions to make sure they understand your objective and how your skills and experience support it. If they don't seem to want to take the time to learn about your talents, aspirations, and values, *RUN!*

Their intention. Hire a person who has your best interest at heart and who truly wants you to succeed, not someone who's taken to writing resumes because they're between jobs and they fancy themselves as a decent writer.

Their personality. Although sometimes doctors with a horrible bedside manner turn out to be the best practitioners, you'll feel more comfortable opening up to someone you get along with. Watch out for anyone who seems too "my way or the highway." You want someone who welcomes your questions and who's happy to explain the rationale behind their recommendations. You have to feel comfortable with everything on the page. Employers understand people typically get help with their resume, but they assume you've approved the content. If I have a client who wants something that goes against my better judgment, I try to keep an open mind (which is totally contrary to my innate inclination) and hear them out. That said, I had one client who insisted on keeping some foolish blather on her resume that I just could not live with. I finally said, "Look, your name is at the top of this page, not mine." Then I leaned in and whispered, "Just don't tell anyone I helped you with this."

Many professional resume writers have a website. Scour through that thing carefully to get a sense of everything I just mentioned. I haven't had a website for resume writing because I work from referrals, but I send prospective clients a document that summarizes my approach, the process we'll go through, and what I'm like to work with. I let them know that writing resumes is aligned with my life's mission, and I craft my clients' resumes with the same care and attention I would for a member of my family. I also advise them that if they're a miserable person or a pain in the ass, they're on their own. The beauty of working for myself is that I can choose to work only with people I think are nice. Anyone who hires me will know exactly what they're in for right up front.

Some prospective clients have asked whether I can guarantee their resume will result in a job offer. Oh, hell, no! Too many factors lie outside my control. You can have a beautiful resume, but if your cover letter is a bloody mess, you probably won't get called for an interview. If you have creepy social skills or talk too much during an interview, no one will want to work with you. The only thing a resume writer can guarantee is they'll put forth their best effort in presenting your value to a prospective employer. If they promise anything beyond that, they're full of crap.

Your objective drives the content and how you present it. That gets especially tricky when you intend to change careers, return to the type of work you did in the past, or downshift into a less demanding role. In those cases, a resume writer who really knows their stuff can be a godsend.

Communicate your brand through social media

As you know, your mere presence communicates your brand through your appearance and the vibe you exude. You may also choose to communicate your brand through social media, and in the business world, LinkedIn is currently where it's at.

Why you want to be on LinkedIn

Do you *have* to be on LinkedIn? Of course not, you're a grown-ass adult—that's totally up to you. I've had many clients who adamantly refused to have any kind of presence on social media due to privacy concerns. One didn't want her crazy ex to know her business. Another woman insisted that LinkedIn is a dating site in disguise because her profile resulted in a deluge of aspiring suitors. (I thought, "Honey, stop. You are not that cute.") I do understand why people are hesitant to put themselves out there, but if you're looking for a job, LinkedIn is a necessary evil. Here's why:

- Hiring managers and recruiters search LinkedIn to find candidates, perhaps even before a position is made public. A strong LinkedIn profile can get their attention, and you may be contacted with a request for your resume.
- LinkedIn has a powerful job board that shows not only open positions, but also displays names of people you know who currently, or in the past, have worked in those companies.
- Your profile allows you to offer a prospective employer insight into who you are as a person, beyond what you have on your resume. This is important since people hire *people*, not resumes.
- LinkedIn provides an easy way to research the companies you're interested in, and again, to see who you know with connections to those companies.

- LinkedIn provides a platform to share articles you've written on your areas of expertise. This is a great way to promote your brand and position yourself as an authority.

Now that I've made such a case for having a LinkedIn profile, I have to tell you… personally, I don't love it. I kind of hate it. I rarely scroll through to see what's going on, and if I do, it's only because I'm procrastinating on something else. The self-promoting posts are fine since that is pretty much the purpose of the site, but so much of what I see seems forced and lacking in authenticity. Most posts are about topics I find boring as hell, and sweet bearded Jesus, how many articles on leadership do people need to share? That said, LinkedIn provides a platform to maintain relationships and communicate privately with people I *do* care about, and that is where I see its value.

Tips on building a strong LinkedIn profile

While a well-developed LinkedIn profile can pique a prospective employer's interest, a poorly written or outdated profile is worse than having no profile at all. Take care when putting yours together. As with resumes, you'll find helpful resources online, so please dig deeper than what I have here. Based on what LinkedIn looks like as I write this, here is how I recommend communicating your personal brand. The platform is pretty intuitive, so don't freak.

Photo. Do you really need a photo? Yes. Without one, people will think the worst. Your photo should reflect your personal brand, so if you fancy yourself as happy and outgoing, don't post a face that belongs on currency. A color headshot with a neutral background is best. Repeat: *head* shot. You may be proud of your rockin' body, but LinkedIn is not the place to show it off. You can have your photo professionally taken if you need it for other purposes, but it's fine to have someone snap a shot with your phone.

Background photo. To reinforce your personal brand and add a little pizzazz to your profile, upload a background photo that represents what you do or gives the feel of your industry. Google "LinkedIn background photos" and you're sure to find something interesting. Don't feel you have to use a stock photo. Upload one of your own, even one that you're in. Just make sure it's relevant, supports your brand, and adheres to LinkedIn's size specifications.

Subhead (under your name). For most people, this is the same heading as their resume or "what you are" in your branding statement. This doesn't have to be super succinct, so feel free to add areas of ability or credentials. Some people say "seeking new opportunities" at the end to communicate their immediate availability.

Profile URL. When you create your profile, the URL currently defaults to a mess of letters and numbers after your name. Since it's a good idea to put a link to your profile in the heading of your resume, you'll want to customize this for a cleaner look.

About. This section should answer the following questions: Who are you? What do you excel at? How are you unique? Why do you love what you do? Where do you hit your home run? The content here is basically the same as the top of your resume but expressed in a conversational tone. Whereas your resume is a technical document, with no voice or use of personal pronouns, LinkedIn is *social* media. People want to see your face and hear your voice and feel as though they know you as a person. You can also add a couple of bulleted accomplishments, but be sure to provide some kind of context to avoid confusion. At the end, list your areas of expertise so you can work in key terms to feed the search engines. Some people attach their resume in this section, but I say generate enough interest in your profile and then let a prospective employer ask for it.

Experience. Provide a quick overview of each position and add the accomplishments you're most proud of. Don't copy and paste every single word from your resume, but make sure the experience you list matches your resume. I recommend using a conversational tone here as well.

Recommendations. Having recommendations could tip the scales on whether you're called for an interview. Ask some people in your professional network—current or former managers, coworkers, vendors, or internal or external customers—to write up something nice about you that's not fiction. Because you solicit these recommendations through LinkedIn, you need to be connected to the people you're hitting up. Keep in mind you're giving someone a task that nobody really wants to do, so make it as easy as possible for those kind souls. Let them know what you'd particularly like them to highlight. Be prepared for someone to ask you to draft your own recommendation for them. That's fine; you'll have more control over the message.

Education. As with your resume, unless you have a recent degree (within the past five years or so), there's no need to include the dates of your education. But, as with your resume, if the year of your degree indicates you're a life-long learner, then go for it.

Connections. The broader your network, the more valuable LinkedIn will be to you. Reach out to current and former coworkers, vendors, customers, and people you know through professional affiliations. Look through the contacts in your cell phone and other forms of social media. Connect only with people you actually know, although you don't have to know them very well. Always add a short personal note to your request to connect.

Other social media platforms

Facebook, Twitter, and Instagram are typically used to share more personal information, and that's where you have to be careful. Prospective employers often check a candidate's social media accounts as part of their screening process to get a sense of who you are as a person. Of course, they may also come across some dirt that could put you out of the running, so don't be stupid about what you post. Tighten the privacy settings on your profile or review your posts and hide or delete the ones that someone could take issue with. That doesn't guarantee the data is completely gone; someone with the know-how and motivation can find anything. If you have an iota of common sense and aren't off-the-charts bizarre, I wouldn't fret too much about employers peeking into your personal life. You could just as easily snoop around their stuff, too.

The way I look at it, social media is an honest representation of who you are. If someone were to look at my social media, they'd see I have certain political views. I swear. I post all kinds of inane observations that normal people, especially somebody's grandmother, would never put out there. I wouldn't show that hand on an interview or lead with it my first day of work, but once people get to know me, they'll figure all that out for themselves. You can't, and shouldn't, completely edit yourself out in the workplace and you're not going to be everybody's cup of tea. Both you, and the prospective employer, will be better off if they know what they're getting before anyone makes a commitment.

9. Rock Your Self-Confidence

YOU HAVE A CLEAR SENSE OF DIRECTION, your resume is ready for prime time, and you feel good about your social media presence. You're ready to get yourself out there.

Stepping into unknown territory can be scary, especially if you've been coasting along on autopilot for years. Although that can be comfortable, we don't learn anything while on autopilot. It isn't stimulating and it can make us lazy. Sometimes a life-changing event such as divorce, a serious illness, or job loss will jolt us out of it, so be thankful if you're leaving autopilot proactively. It's much easier to reflect, re-evaluate, and plan when you haven't been blindsided.

Ditching autopilot for the path to a new and better life will occasionally lead you outside your comfort zone. You may reach out to someone you don't know very well and ask if they'll meet you for coffee. You might strike up a conversation with a stranger at a networking gathering. Maybe you'll go on an interview for the first time since forever and then be faced with having to negotiate an offer of employment.

As a comedian, I leave my comfort zone every time I walk on stage. It still doesn't come easy. I have struggled with stage fright since my first open mic in 2003, and to this day, my stomach churns before every single show. Each "first" has brought a new level of anxiety—the first time I performed for hundreds of people, the first time I knew a celebrity would be in the audience, the first time I opened for a celebrity. I've learned to welcome that anxiety because each new milestone is a sign that I'm getting better and so are the opportunities that come to me. Many performers never completely lose stage fright, and I know I'll never get over it entirely. I accept pre-show diarrhea as part of the package. The rewards make it all worthwhile.

You have to step out of your comfort zone now and then, even if it (literally) scares the crap out of you. You may have to force yourself, but once you're out there you'll realize three things: 1) Whatever you did wasn't that scary after all, 2) You feel a fantastic sense of pride, and 3) Your comfort zone has expanded, which means you can now do more with ease. Or at least with a little less anxiety. That's growth.

Tips for projecting self-confidence

What is self-confidence, anyway? The term is often used interchangeably with self-esteem, but they're two different animals. One is about value and the other is about trust. Self-esteem is the *value* you place on your self-worth. It's the relationship you have with yourself; it's knowing who you are and liking that person. Think of self-confidence as the *trust* you have in your abilities, your personal fortitude, and your sense of judgment. It's possible to have high self-esteem and low self-confidence. For example, you can have great self-esteem, meaning you like and value who you are, but lack the confidence to leave your job for something new because you don't trust your ability to navigate that unknown territory. On the flip side, someone can have high self-confidence and low self-esteem. You can be a fantastic performer, playing to an audience with great confidence, yet offstage harbor deep-seated feelings of inadequacy.

When you lack self-confidence, you constantly doubt yourself and wonder, *Am I doing this right? Should I have said that? Am I functioning okay?* Everyone experiences some degree of self-doubt, which is good because otherwise you'd be a total douche. Have you ever noticed that douches seem incredibly self-confident?

That's because they have no self-doubt to keep them in check. Nor do they have an accurate perception of how they're coming across. I guarantee the more douchey a person is, the lower their self-esteem. Their bravado is all an act; they're trying to convince themselves of their self-worth as much as they're trying to convince you.

So having a little bit of self-doubt and experiencing the anxiety it can provoke isn't entirely bad. It means you want to do a good job; you care. Communication expert Dale Carnegie once said, "Far worse than the fear of doing poorly is the assumption of doing well." I've seen this with fellow comics. The ones so sure of themselves that feel it's okay to smoke a dube and down another beer before hitting the stage are sure to suck. However, too much anxiety can impede our ability to perform well or paralyze us from taking any action at all. How do you find the balance between "douche" and "basket case"? I think it comes down to three things: 1) Being yourself, 2) Knowing your stuff, and 3) Loving yourself and the stuff you have to offer.

Be the real you

We hear so much about personal empowerment in the context of setting and achieving goals, but real personal power comes from having the courage to be YOU. As much as the words "authentic self" make me want to gag, it's important to know who you are at your core and to consciously live as that person. Your degree of authenticity is measured by the alignment of who you are on the inside with the person you present to the outside world.

As children we start out being perfectly authentic. We don't know any other way to be. Then as time goes on, the experiences of life start shifting our behavior and perspectives. We cave in to social pressures to look or act a certain way. We say things to please others and to fit in with the crowd. As we grow into adulthood, we start to wear masks and play roles that dictate how we're supposed to act, including in the workplace, where to some degree one's livelihood is tied to the ability to conform. If we're not careful, years pass and we all but lose the person at the center of who we are.

Then as we head into AARP territory, we start to realize how much energy we've spent playing those roles and we wonder whether the payoff was worth the weariness. With every passing day, we're more inclined to proclaim, "Like it or not, I am who I am!" That's why I find older people so endearing and entertaining—

they've abandoned the notion of keeping up the act and fearlessly project their authenticity. My mother takes that a wee bit too far. She'll watch a woman walk through a crowded restaurant and bark, "What the hell is *she* wearing?" Well, Mom, I'll tell you what she's not wearing: a hearing aid. That filter is off for good.

As you can imagine, parenting styles can influence one's self-esteem. My siblings and I are lucky. Our mother would smother us kids with affection, hugging us to the point where we literally couldn't breathe. She'd squeeze us tightly and tell us we were "so beautiful" and "so smart" and she was the luckiest mother on earth. I believed her; it didn't cross my mind that she would be lying. But don't get me wrong, she kept us in check so we wouldn't get too full of ourselves. One day when I was about eight or nine, I looked out the window and asked, "Is the air blowing the trees around, or are the trees moving and that's what is making it windy?" Mothers today would clasp their hands with glee and exclaim, "My, what a delightful perspective you have!" But her response was, "Jesus Christ, that's the stupidest goddamn question I ever heard."

No matter what kind of upbringing you had, no matter how much you've struggled with self-esteem or self-confidence issues in the past, you can commit right now to improving both. The first step is to get back in touch with your authentic self, and having done the exercises in the previous chapters, you've already made huge strides. You've identified what brings you joy, where your values lie, the areas where you excel, and the talents you intend to share with the world. You weren't creating fiction—that's authentic stuff you wrote down. With all my heart, I hope you like who that person is.

To make sure you're living authentically, always live close to the truth and strive to express the truth in the kindest way possible. Intend to be more genuine and to act on your genuine nature. This means you replace what you *should* do with what you *want* to do and make choices that put YOU first. Back in the second chapter about living with joy, we talked about the importance of saying no. Remind yourself that "No" is a complete sentence that does not require further explanation. Be more aware of when you're aligned with your authenticity and when you're not, and hold yourself accountable to act in ways that are consistent with your values.

Your sense of authenticity builds your self-esteem, which affects the strength of your self-confidence. Read that again.

Living authentically liberates you from the pressure of being someone you just can't be. You feel more invigorated because wearing masks takes a lot of energy. I think about the god-awful plastic masks that kids growing up in the 1960s wore on Halloween. I could hardly see because the eye holes were never lined up correctly, and I was always messing with the thing until the cheap rubber band that was supposed to hold it to my head finally broke. And while I was disappointed that I no longer looked like Casper the Friendly Ghost, I was just as happy to no longer fight with that goddamn mask. I've felt the same frustration and drain of energy from some of the corporate masks I've worn.

Besides being able to chuck the mask, living authentically offers many other benefits. You find it easier to make decisions since you simply choose the option that's in line with your truth. People like hanging with you. They appreciate not having to second guess where you're coming from. They see how comfortable you are being yourself, and in turn they feel comfortable being themselves around you. You become less judgmental and more forgiving of yourself as well as other people who give off the "authentic" vibe. You enjoy people more and become more inquisitive. You approach strangers with an eagerness to hear what they're all about. You don't compare yourself to others because you know everybody is one of a kind. You don't care too much whether people like you or not. You like yourself, and that's all that matters.

Be at peace with your looks

Being at peace with your looks means accepting what you perceive as imperfections. The key words are "what you perceive." I can look in the mirror and identify ten things that are "wrong," and no matter how many times my husband says, "No, Linda, one eye is *not* bigger than the other," I never truly believe him.

We're too fat, too skinny, not muscular enough. Our boobs and ass aren't the right size, our stomach is flabby, our arms aren't toned, our legs are too short… I could go on. I once visited a 102-year-old woman in a nursing home and during a lull in our conversation, she glanced down and pointed to an age spot on her forearm. "I hate this thing," she said. That's when I realized it's never going to end.

I've been complaining about my thin, crappy hair since junior high, and have spent decades and a fortune on miracle hair products trying to get the ten hairs on my head look like twenty. People remark that I have "baby" hair. No, this is my adult hair; my baby hair was a comb-over. I got that from my father. One time Mike tried to comfort me by saying, "Honey, your hair looks fine," to which I snarled, "Yes, I have fine hair. That's kind of the whole problem. Why do you have to be such a dick about it?"

Weight is another issue a lot of us struggle with, often by choice. If I weighed now what I did when I first started complaining about my weight, I'd be horribly sick with maybe two weeks to live. Recently I met a woman my age who ever-so-casually mentioned she weighs the same as she did in high school. My knee-jerk reaction was *bitch!* But then I thought, at forty pounds heavier than when I was seventeen, I am literally the size of my high school self and my second-grade self combined into one incredible person. That's pretty impressive.

I know it's hard, but try not to be too critical of how you look. People don't see you as you do, and they don't care nearly as much, if at all. I have never thought I'd have a better time with anyone or hold them closer to my heart if only they'd lose a few pounds. Nobody would like me more if I had thick hair. In fact, they'd probably hate me. I'm pretty full of myself now; I'd be unbearable flaunting a luxurious mane.

Society in general and advertisers in particular do a number on us by setting impossible standards for how we think we should look. Currently, the quest for perfect eyebrows is fueling a billion-dollar industry of products and procedures. I came across an ad on Facebook that said, "Are your eyebrows making you old?" No, it's my sagging jawline and chicken neck, and F-U for asking. I'd be singing hallelujah if I looked in the mirror and thought my hair looks good, my face looks good, my stomach flab is gone, both eyes are the same size… I guess we're down to the eyebrows. If there's something about your looks that really, really brings you down and truly affects your self-esteem, I say there's nothing wrong with doing something about it. Cosmetic work is one of the few things I think is okay to finance, as long as you need it in real life and you're not being nutty or vain.

Watch your posture

The way you carry yourself communicates so much about your sense of self. Remember this: People treat you exactly how you tell them to. Good posture proclaims, "You'd be crazy to mess with me!" A commanding posture is especially important if you're in a situation where you need to project a sense of authority, like when you're interviewing or returning an outfit to Target without a receipt. People don't say no to someone with perfect posture.

We can dye our hair, wear tinted contact lenses, whiten our teeth, and spend a fortune on eyebrows, but poor posture cannot be disguised or transformed cosmetically. Forget the ego issues, though, and let's talk about the physical consequences. Degeneration of the spinal column affects the health of every system in your body. When the back becomes rounded, it compresses the chest, which restricts breathing and the flow of blood. This limits the amount of oxygen the cells in your body receives and contributes to cardiovascular disease and other health issues, including those related to digestion and elimination. No one wants problems like that.

Try this: Stand straight and pull your shoulders back and down. Exaggerate this stance to really sense how that feels. Imagine a string at the crown of your head that's being pulled up to the sky. With your shoulders back and down and your head lifting, elongate your spine. Visualize creating space between each vertebra. Tighten your abdominal muscles in and pull them up as if you're lying on your bed trying to pull up the zipper on super tight jeans. Now smile. This is your new baseline.

Consciously make a point to maintain this posture whether you're sitting, standing, or walking. Remind yourself to do this at least a million times a day. Eventually, the practice will seep into your subconscious mind and perfect posture will become second nature. Wherever you are, whatever you're doing, let this be your mantra: "Shoulders back and down, head high."

I believe yoga is a fantastic way to improve not only your posture, but your overall physical and mental health. Please don't assume yoga is only for super-spiritual, metaphysical, clean-living vegetarians. I used to teach yoga and I'll tell you right now, I was a meat-eatin', beer-drinkin', swearin' type of yoga teacher, and there's an element of the yoga culture that annoys the hell out of me.

Pick up a yoga magazine. Chances are the cover is graced by a 105-pound model in a bizarre Cirque du Soleil contortion. That doesn't exactly scream, "Yoga is easy; anyone can do it!" And if you look through the ads, you'll see everything costs a fortune—the special yoga apparel, the props, the yoga retreats... I get pissed about the elitism associated with yoga. Yoga's not meant to be esoteric—it should be accessible to the masses—and it doesn't have to cost a lot. All you need is comfortable clothes and a ten-dollar sticky mat from Walmart. And anyone really *can* do yoga.

The beauty of yoga is that whatever you do is perfect as long as your actions don't lead you toward pain or fear. If you're holding a posture, or *asana*, and start to feel discomfort, you simply ease back a bit. You never press through. If you're afraid to attempt a posture, don't do it. Unlike in theatre or dance classes, we're not creating something for others to look at; there's no performance aspect or sense of competition. You honor where you are in the present moment and accept that you're perfect.

So how do you find a yoga class that's right for you? Yoga teachers are like snowflakes—no two are alike. Just as there are several varieties of hatha yoga, there are countless approaches to teaching. Almost every yoga studio allows you to take a class on a drop-in basis; my advice is to drop in on several. If you don't connect with what's going on, take another class. But don't give up on yoga altogether. And you don't have to take classes forever. Once you've learned several asanas, you can practice yoga on your own at home by yourself or with YouTube videos.

My first yoga teacher used to say, "You're as young as your spine." Believe it. Yoga is all about maintaining the health and integrity of the spine. It's the closest thing we have to a real-life Fountain of Youth.

Act "as if"

Acting "as if" is a technique I started using in college to psych myself up. I had a professor who exuded amazing confidence, and when I had to give presentations, I'd channel her style. These days I act as if I'm the best dancer in my Zumba class. I know I'm doing the steps completely wrong, but I do them with such conviction that everyone else thinks *they're* out of step. Including the teacher. Even if you're not feeling particularly sure of yourself, act as if you're the most confident person in the world.

Try this: Think of someone whose confidence you admire. What about that person's posture or way of speaking conveys self-confidence? Assume that person's attributes and act as if you already *are* in the position to which you aspire. Try out that confident version of yourself in your next social situation or boring work meeting.

Get a personal theme song

Remember Julie Andrews in *The Sound of Music* belting out "I Have Confidence" while skipping on her way to meet the captain and seven children? Personal theme songs are a lot of fun and I swear they work. I have two, but I can't tell you what they are. They're called *personal* theme songs for a reason.

Try this: Think of a confidence-building song that puts a bounce in your step. Play the song in your head while you're walking out to the mailbox or strutting down the beer aisle in the grocery store. Remember to keep your shoulders back and down, head high. You can't help but feel a bit ridiculous, but don't worry, no one will ever know why.

Overcoming "Yeah, but" fears

Everyone is afraid of something. I will abandon a full cart of groceries at Costco if I see a bird in the rafters, and one time I freaked out, tripping over all Mike's shit in the garage, because I thought a bird was in there. Thankfully, it turned out to be an eyeball floater. Anyway, maybe you're afraid of heights or spiders or the most common fear of all: public speaking. The fears that erode our confidence and stop us from getting what we want are the ones I want to address here. Let's frame them as "Yeah, buts…"

Yeah, but what will people think?

You can't rock the self-confidence if you're always worrying about what people will think. It's common to fear the judgment or disapproval of others, and I'd love to be able to say, "Who gives a crap what people think?" but such a cavalier attitude is unrealistic and will not serve you well. We *should* care what people think. We just need to decipher and use the helpful feedback we get and ignore the rest, especially feedback that's rooted in someone's ego and insecurities.

This book is a hundred times better because of the input I've received from my test readers. They've caught mistakes I missed and brought up issues that never would have occurred to me. They've suggested edits that reduced ambiguity and significantly strengthened my message. Sometimes I considered their input but decided to keep the text as it was. Just as your name is on your resume, my name is on this book. Therefore, readers assume everything in here reflects choices made by me, not someone else. If a reviewer on Amazon says, "I don't like the way the author structured Chapter 5," I can't respond with, "Oh, one of my test readers suggested that. I didn't agree, but I went with it anyway."

As of right now my memoir, *Bastard Husband: A Love Story,* has over a hundred reviews on Amazon. Trust me, they're not all spectacular.

"Boring... I did not even finish it. Was dumb and ridicules [sic]. I would not recommend to even my best friend who really has a bastard husband."

"If you enjoy seeing the F word over and over... Then this book is for you. The author is educated so presumably intelligent but is unable to express herself without that word. Humerous [sic] but silly. Lots of worthwhile books out there. This isn't one."

"Funny, but... You really just end up wanting the main character to buck up and stop milling [sic] over her last marriage... and act her age."

"No wonder her husband drank. He could do no right, she can do no wrong."

I file this feedback under "You can't please everybody." Except for digging up these reviews to include here, I haven't given them a second thought. What I often think about is the email I received from a woman in Saudi Arabia who said my story made her laugh for the first time she could remember.

After the book you're holding is out in circulation, rest assured some readers will not only rip it to shreds, but they'll relish every second doing it. I imagine the reviews looming in my future:

"She uses too much slang and cliches, and her voice is very immature for someone her age."

No argument there.

"She says the word 'shit' 26 times, which is very unprofessional."

You wouldn't believe how many "shits" I took out.

"She devotes only one paragraph to starting your own business."

That is correct. I'm not an expert on that topic, which is also why I don't advise people on vegetarian cooking or how to run a marathon.

Chapter 9. Rock Your Self-Confidence

Some readers will disagree with my approach to writing resumes and some will take issue with my advice for negotiating a higher salary and some will hate everything about me. If those critics have a more pleasing personality or better advice to offer, they can direct readers to their own books. They won't stop me. As I write each word, do I think of the people who will never warm up to me? Of course not. I think of Areej in Saudi Arabia.

☙❧

Some of us have parents whose opinions weigh heavily on our decision-making scales. No matter how old we get, if we're lucky enough to still have our parents, we crave their approval and can't bear the thought of disappointing them. Every (good) parent wants the best for their kids, but sometimes their most loving intentions can be misaligned with their children's desires. This is especially problematic if these "children" are fifty-year-old adults. I've worked with too many clients who followed a career path that satisfied their parents' aspirations instead of their own. Those who immediately come to mind are the quality assurance software tester who wished he'd gone to college for musical theater and the financial analyst who, upon being let go from a job she held for decades, finally pursued her dream of becoming an interior designer.

For twenty-three years, my father sold life insurance for the same company that both his father and his grandfather did. It's safe to say that selling insurance was nothing Dad loved or particularly excelled at, and it wasn't until after my grandfather died that he finally got out of that business. He became a city bus driver and was never happier. To me, that was a perfect career choice for him—my father loved to drive, and with his gregarious personality and sense of humor, he enjoyed entertaining his passengers with his Yogi Berra-style one liners. I think the highlight of his career was when he was selected to be photographed behind the wheel as part of the Capital District Transit Authority's promotional campaign. Smart move—if anyone looked like the quintessential bus driver, he did. I can still picture Dad nodding and pointing as he drove by his image on billboards plastered all over the Albany metro area.

Maybe my grandfather would have disapproved of his son trading in a business suit for a bus driver's uniform. Or maybe not. Maybe my grandfather also hated selling insurance but retired from the company because that's what *his* father wanted. Unfortunately, Dad didn't live long enough to retire. He died in 1999 at age sixty-five while vacationing in Florida with his girlfriend. (He and my mother were divorced by then or he would have died when he got *back* from vacation with his girlfriend.) My sister Lori had stored one of the old billboards in her garage, and we displayed it at his wake. It was both comforting and fun to watch people solemnly enter the viewing room at the funeral home and then crack up when they saw his smiling face, larger than life.

People often end up pursuing the same careers as their parents. There's no mystery in that; we offer advice based on what we know. If you're a parent or other influencer, please don't march your kids down a path only because it's the one you followed or push them into a computer science degree when they show zero interest in technology. Allow them to choose a direction that reflects *their* passion, not yours.

As much as you'd like to have your parents' approval, you may not get it. In that case, I hope you have the fortitude to press on and follow your heart. (That's going to be a lot harder if your folks are paying your cell phone bill.) Your parents don't necessarily have to support your desires, but they do have to love you no matter what. If they withhold their love because of your career decision, then when the time comes, I suggest you pick out the crappiest nursing home you can find.

What other people think is important only to the degree that their feedback supports your objective. I believe the best feedback is the feedback you agree with. You might not agree right away; sometimes you have to mull over what you hear before it makes sense and rings true. When you value your sense of self and trust your worthiness, you can better assess the opinions of others, their motivations, and your own reactions to what they say. The people offering you advice don't know you as well as you know yourself. They probably don't know *themselves* that well. Only you know what's right for you.

You might not want to share your aspirations until you've thought them through a bit. Except for a couple of people closest to me, I didn't tell anyone back East I was planning to do my first open mic. Since I was never the class clown or life of the party, nobody would have believed me anyway. Even after I'd been doing comedy for years, friends from high school have said, "No offense, Linda, but I don't remember you being funny." You don't have to share your plans with anyone except the people who are in a position to help you or offer support. Leave your skeptical and dream-killing friends out of the loop. Identify the people whose opinions you respect, who know the territory, and who won't try to influence you with their own biases and fears. It's hard to believe, but some people secretly may not want to see you do well. Your success could remind them of what they're not accomplishing and pose a threat to their egos. Instead of letting any haters immobilize you, think of how annoyed they'll be by your great success.

Yeah, but I'm too old

So often I've heard clients say, "I'm (however many) years old. Who's going to hire me?" I want to reply, "Nobody! You sound like a bitter old person." Yet their concerns of being passed over for opportunities because of age are not without warrant. Regardless of what the laws say, prejudicial hiring practices are not a thing of the past. Age discrimination exists, as does discrimination based on color, religion, disability and sex, the latter encompassing gender identity, sexual orientation, and pregnancy.

So yes, you could experience a certain degree of unjust bias because of your age. Although an employer isn't going to come out and say, "We'd prefer to hire someone who's not so… vintage," people in positions with hiring power can hold some pretty messed up perceptions. They may not see you fitting into their company's youthful organizational culture. They may wonder whether you'll be able to take direction from someone younger than you or whether you'll have the energy to keep up. They may fear you're stuck in your ways and aren't open to learning new things. In the seventies, my grandfather got a hand-held calculator for Christmas. He didn't trust it and would sit there scribbling out long division to check its accuracy. His head would explode if he saw what we have in our pockets today.

I don't know for sure if I've ever experienced age discrimination in the corporate world. I have wondered, though. In my early days in Las Vegas, I had two interviews and was asked to come back to do a mock training presentation for a hotel and casino with a rock and roll theme. I felt quite encouraged until… crickets. My phone calls weren't returned, my "Hey, just checking in" emails received no response. At the time, I was in my mid-forties and despite fancying myself as quite hip and happening, it did occur to me that maybe I was being passed over for the job because they thought I was too long in the tooth. I'll never know for sure.

Do Want You Want

This I do know. A couple of years ago one of my comedian friends mentioned he'd been approached by a booker in a local club who was looking for a "young and hot" female comic. Although in the right lighting I'm pretty okay looking and have a certain amount of sex appeal left in me, the conversation did not end with, "So I gave him your name." There's no disputing that I'm not a young comic, but not being considered because of my age and assumed un-hotness gave me a bit of a jolt. I was annoyed for a nanosecond and then figured, who the hell cares? Do I want to work for somebody whose criteria is young and hot instead of actually being funny? My response would be the same had I been passed up for a corporate position because of my age. *Fine, good luck. NEXT!*

As with everything in life, determine what's within your control and what's not. Work on the stuff that is and let go of everything else. It's not within your control if someone has a mindset that's hell-bent on hiring a younger person, and in the corporate world, age is probably not the issue as much an employer's unwillingness to compensate "more mature" workers for the years of experience they bring. Companies don't necessarily want someone younger; they want someone cheaper. That's not within your control, so that's not your problem. That particular opportunity is not meant to be.

I admit that for some career choices, the ship has sailed. Even if you're as young as twenty, it's too late to pursue a career as a professional football player. But you may be able to work for the NFL and get your football fix in some other role. I'm never going to be a ballerina, but I get my dance fix by taking lessons and following along with YouTube videos. Better to focus on what you *can* do than lament what you're too late for. I got into comedy when I was forty-six, which in that world is considered ancient. As long as I can speak properly, I should be able to perform as long as I want. Joan Rivers was hilarious until the day she died at age eighty-one. Phyllis Diller gave her final performance in Las Vegas in 2002, when she was in her mid-eighties. Funny is funny, and age has nothing to do with it.

How not to seem old:

As I said before, people treat you exactly the way you tell them to. If you present yourself as old, people will treat you as such. Here are my suggestions for keeping that old-person vibe in check.

Stand up straight. The rounding of the spine is *the* most visible sign of aging. If it's hard for you to stand up straight, make it a point to work on your posture. I've already told you how to do that.

Don't go moaning about your aches and pains. I ache every day, not because I'm old, but because I take four dance classes a week. And for God's sake, don't hold your lower lumbar and grunt when you bend down to pick something up. Keep those noises to yourself. Even if you have health issues, project vitality the best you can.

Don't complain about the younger generation. I know it's hard for some people my age to understand how a twenty-eight-year-old could still live with their parents and have them pay for their car insurance. In some ways it does seem that adolescence lasts forever and thirty is the new ten. Every generation has its challenges, whether posed by wartime, economic conditions, social unrest, or a global health pandemic. Today's young people are faced with issues that no one my age has had to deal with. The "duck and cover" drills we did in the 60s to protect us from the Soviets can't compare with the training children go through to minimize casualties from an active shooter *in their classrooms*. And I can't even begin to wrap my head around the pressures of being a teen or pre-teen in the age of social media.

It's not cool to bash the younger generations about their sense of entitlement. I think young people have a point. They want things like work-life balance, something baby boomers would have welcomed, but we didn't have the guts to ask for. That's because the work ethic we inherited from our parents was practically draconian. I can imagine my father's take on it: *Work-life balance? You're lucky you have a goddamn job!*

We hear that we live in a youth-obsessed culture, but I think there's never been a better time to be older. I grew up hearing the Woodstock-era mantra, "Never trust anyone over thirty." *Thirty*. I'm generalizing, but as a whole, young people are wonderfully accepting and inclusive. Most of us today enjoy a social life that's delightfully intergenerational. My friends range from their twenties to their eighties. Nobody cares how old anybody is.

No matter what your age, strike up a conversation with somebody from a different generation or a different culture. Learn what they do for fun, what's important to them, what they worry about, and how they handle what life throws at them. But let's not put them down—that just makes us seem out of touch.

Don't be overly sensitive about your age. Own it; age is nothing to apologize for. I tell anyone who will listen how old I am so they can see what someone in their sixties looks like. I want younger people to see that those of us my age and beyond can be funny and vibrant and a source of knowledge and support. For people in their forties and fifties, I hope to allay whatever fears they may have of getting older. And I hope to inspire my fellow senior discount lovers to create an Act III that surpasses their wildest dreams.

Although I don't recommend stating on your resume that you started your first job in 1982, don't go crazy trying to hide your age. If your LinkedIn photo doesn't give it away, your name might. "Linda" was the most popular girl's name in America from 1947-1952. It was still riding high when I made the scene in 1957—there were four Lindas in my class. Half the women in my 55+ community are named Linda. I once gave my name to a barista at Starbucks, and despite my freakishly youthful appearance, the kid exclaimed, "That's my grandma's name!" No one under fifty is named Linda except this one cashier I met in World Market. Upon noticing her name tag, I remarked, "Wow, I've never met a young Linda." She rolled her eyes and said, "My parents named me after Linda Ronstadt." Names have a way of coming back in style, though—we're currently seeing a revival of "nursing home" names like Mabel, Evelyn, and Hazel (my granddaughter's name). Maybe someday Linda will be retro-cool, but until then, it screams Boomer. Not that there's anything wrong with it.

Look in the mirror. How can you improve on what you see? I should be the last person to give advice about hair, but I will anyway. You certainly don't have to get rid of the gray to project a youthful impression, but if you do dye your hair, throw in some highlights. That will give it depth and the appearance of volume, especially if you have fine, thin hair like mine. And for the love of all things holy, don't go walking around with those 80s-style bangs that look like a bird's nest sitting on your forehead.

Speaking of hair, every self-respecting woman over forty should own tweezers and a 10x magnifying mirror so you don't go walking around looking like ZZ Top. And guys, you owe the world the same consideration. Tame those crazy "guy brows," and whatever you do, trim that nose hair. When I see a man with wild nose or ear hair, I conclude either he's blind or his wife hates him.

As far as clothes go, pick out something a little jazzy. Add a splash of color. (I'm telling myself that as well since everything I own is black.) Spice yourself up with some funky jewelry. The next time you shop for eyeglasses, have a young friend or relative help you pick out something hip. You have to be you, though. Don't buy anything you're not comfortable with or that's not really your style. Above all, make sure whatever you wear brings you joy. Ignore those articles that tell you what not to wear after you've reached a certain age. Whoever writes that crap can kiss my ass. I'll wear miniskirts until I'm damn good and ready to give them up. The legs are the last to go.

℘⃝

Your age is one of those things you (honestly) can't change, but how you approach it is up to you. You can choose to embrace getting older, enjoy it, and even use it to your advantage. I whip out that AARP card for my ten percent discount at Outback faster than you can say, "Crikey!" I never wish I were younger or that I could go back to a previous time in life. I'm thrilled that my days of buying tampons and supervising a fifth-grade science project are way behind me. Every age has its advantages, and one of the reasons why getting older rocks is that it's easier to instill credibility. We really do get wiser every day. I wouldn't be able to advise executives on how to position themselves for the next step in their careers if I were thirty years younger. I was an idiot back then.

Yeah, but what if I'm rejected?

I hate to break it to you, but rejection is an inevitable fact of life. I learned that at age nine, when my favorite jokes I'd sent to Johnny Carson were returned unopened. Your loss, Johnny. They were freakin' brilliant. Comedy gold.

Not to sound negative, but as you explore and pursue a new path, not everything will go your way. A former coworker doesn't respond to your request for a LinkedIn recommendation. A networking contact keeps putting off a date to get together for coffee. You're not selected to join a company after getting all dolled up and schlepping across town three times for an interview. I understand the frustration. A job search is like a game that's structured with the odds stacked against you. But just by being willing to play, you significantly increase the likelihood of having a happier life. So deal yourself in.

When you feel you've been rejected, your imagination begs to go wild and make up reasons as to why. Limit your thinking to what you actually know for sure. For example, let's say two weeks have passed since you reached out to someone in your network and you haven't heard anything back. You can choose to feel hurt and insecure and convince yourself that you suck as a person and who the hell are you anyway to think you're so important to deserve a spot on their calendar? Or you can choose to understand that people get a billion emails a day and are crazy busy and they go on vacation and have family emergencies. Maybe they would welcome another email or text to remind them of your initial outreach. You might also choose to believe it's okay if they never get back to you at all because you'll find some other way to get the information you were seeking from them. Don't go crazy making up fantasy scenarios. You don't know what you don't know.

The ability to handle rejection relates to the expectations you set and how you respond to what you perceive. The more you're attached to a particular outcome, the more you feel things *have* to work out a particular way. That will leave you open to disappointment and angst. Do your best—work on whatever is in your control—and trust that the universe unfolds in divine order. But don't be immobilized by the fear of not being what somebody's looking for.

CHAPTER 9. ROCK YOUR SELF-CONFIDENCE

Yeah, but what if I suck?

Oh, good God, you're not going to suck. Need I remind you *again* about all the self-assessment work you did? Nonetheless, here are some truths to keep in mind when you're making yourself crazy with self-doubt.

You can't expect perfection right out of the gate. No one is great at anything the first time they do it, but if you stick with it and don't give up, you're sure to get better. When I started doing Zumba, I looked like a stripper being electrocuted. Now I look like I'm just having mild convulsions. My first stand-up performance was pretty decent (considering), but it doesn't compare to my later sets. And the first pages of what would become *Bastard Husband: A Love Story* looked nothing like what ended up in print. The same goes for the book you're holding right now. It was once a bloody mess.

It's easy to talk ourselves out of working toward a goal when the expectation of perfection looms overhead. And so we give up before we take the first step. We let the vision die without giving it a chance. Don't put off starting a project or going down a path because you're afraid you won't execute it perfectly. Over time, what you do will evolve into what you want it to be, as long as you continue to work on it. Plow through the doubt and fear and remember that perfection is the enemy of progress.

You can't hit it out of the park every time. Personally, I hate this realization. I want a home run or nothing, but that's just not realistic, especially when it comes to performing stand-up. Every comic, no matter how seasoned, occasionally has an off night and I've certainly done my share of sets that were the longest twenty or forty minutes of my life. No matter how well prepared I am and no matter how much I love my material and can't wait to share it with the audience, I face the possibility of bombing every time I take the stage. Whereas writers, visual artists, and musicians can assess their creations before deciding which will go public, comedians determine whether a new bit will go over or fall flat only through full-frontal exposure to a room of people. And when we do have an off night, or flat-out bomb, that one set may be the only impression a person may ever have. I could have the flu, receive some bad news on the way to the gig… doesn't matter. *Yeah, I saw Linda Lou perform six years ago. She was terrible.* If they never see me perform again, that crappy set they caught will be my legacy in their minds. Yet we live to get back up there. Comedians have balls of steel. If only we had stomachs of steel.

There will always be someone who does it better than you. The ego would love for you to feel threatened and intimidated by other people's talents. Instead, choose to be inspired by them. Study these individuals. Identify their best practices and integrate them into how you express what you do. The universe is abundant; there's enough talent to go around for everyone. You don't have to be the Michael Jordan or Meryl Streep of your niche to be successful and happy.

Yeah, but what if it doesn't work out?

Nobody can guarantee your plan will work out the way you envision, but I can't imagine why it wouldn't. You didn't spin a wheel and land on "Be a veterinary assistant." You arrived at the decision to pursue your desire methodically and through thoughtful introspection. If you've done your due diligence, including your financial reality check, you're almost sure to succeed.

Still, the fear of making a mistake can play with your mind. I understand, but nobody gets through life without taking a misstep now and then. Unless you're doing neurosurgery or a colonoscopy, it's no big deal. This may be a shock, but if you take a job that doesn't work out, you don't have to stay in it for the rest of your life. Once you finish this book, you'll have the know-how to go find yourself something else.

If it turns out you're not happy with the direction you took and you feel you've made a huge mistake, remember that no experience is ever wasted. Some good can come out of even the biggest cluster. Humor writer David Sedaris says, "In time, everything is funny." The best stories come from when things go wrong, so maybe someday you'll get a good laugh. We live and learn. Proceed.

Yeah, but success frightens me, too

Some people find this concept hard to understand—how can you be afraid to succeed? Do you fear your distant cousin Eddie Griswold will be knocking at your door to hit you up for money or you'll lose friends because they can't contain their jealousy? Do you dread paying taxes in the billionaire bracket? Is that what's stopping you?

A fear of success could be rooted in a few different areas. You may feel what's known as imposter syndrome, where despite the evidence of your competence and achievements, you feel you've fooled people into believing you're actually good at what you do. You attribute your achievements to luck, rather than skill. You feel you don't deserve the rewards resulting from your achievements or if things get too good, something terrible will happen. You can't allow yourself to be *that* happy. Life can't go *that* well. Maybe you secretly don't want to do well because the thought of what the next level of success would require is overwhelming to you. If out of nowhere I got a call to do my own Netflix special, I'd be a blotchy mess and would have to triple the dosage of my blood pressure medicine.

Please believe you deserve the riches, the accolades, and the sense of accomplishment you get from all your hard work. Believe you'll find a way to handle whatever is required in the next level of success.

ဢ০ে

That's the end of my pep talk. Are you ready to get yourself out there? You don't have to; it's entirely up to you. If you don't make an effort to change, I would assume you're either happy where you are or you're happy being unhappy where you are, which would be a shame.

People always say they wish they hadn't waited so long to start something new. Let go of any lingering insecurities. You can do it.

10. Get Yourself Out There

OKAY, IT'S TIME to let the world know how awesome you are. In this chapter, we'll go over the various aspects of networking and approaching companies, either directly or in response to job postings. Let's make things happen.

Building and tapping into your network

Everything you read about the job search tells you it's all about networking and that you're most likely to get your next position through a referral from someone you know. Believe it. There's no doubt that making connections and cultivating relationships will enhance your chances of getting to wherever you want to be.

Why you may hate the thought of networking

The way networking is touted, you'd think it was the most natural thing to do. In a way, it is. You network informally all the time. You think nothing of asking your friends how they like their dentist or mechanic or whether they can recommend an inexpensive weekend getaway. We're used to tapping into the knowledge and experience of others. Yet many people have told me that when it comes to their job search, they're not comfortable networking. Others won't admit to that; they just avoid it. I understand why.

You think of those dreadful networking mixers. Networking gets a bad rap because we associate the word with those awful events where you smile and "work the room" as you press business cards into people's hands. You know how I tell you to live authentically and express your truth? Here's one of my truths: I hate those things.

Now and then in my last job I'd have to attend a networking mixer or some other after-hours function for professionals in human resources. Here's how it invariably went down. After checking in with some overly enthusiastic greeter who sizes me up with a three-second scan, I make a beeline for the bar and order myself a beer. "Save the wine for the ladies," I joke to the bartender, the coolest person in the place. With a shitty light beer in hand because somebody decided people in business can't be trusted with Guinness, I turn on my radar for other shrinking violets who look like they, too, detest superficial schmoozing. Before I can spot my fellow corporate misfits, someone approaches me with the predictable "What do you do?" and "What company are you with?" ice breakers. As I deliver my canned responses, their eyes scan the room, assessing the scene in search of someone… else. Soon they excuse themselves with the obligatory "Nice to meet you." From there, I might position myself awkwardly on the fringe of a group, not really listening since I have zero intention of chiming in. I nod and smile as I plan my escape. I spy a place to abandon my warm, and now even shittier, beer and slowly back away, my absence unnoticed, before rushing to the exit like a ten-year-old who's snitched a Kit-Kat from a 7-Eleven.

I've painted a pretty negative picture, but that's been my experience and I know I'm not the only one. Keep in mind I consider myself to be confident, friendly, and outgoing. I can't imagine what that scene would be like for someone who's introverted. And I'm passionate about what I do! You'd think I'd love to spread the word about the joy of helping people map out their work lives. Nope. That scene isn't the right forum for me. Don't feel bad if it's not for you, either.

The good news is you can reap the benefits of networking in other group settings. Instead of those torturous mixers, look for training sessions or free lectures on topics that interest you. Those gatherings will be less awkward since they're structured around a focal point of attention. You'll be with like-minded people, so do make it a point to get to know the folks around you. Exchange business cards and encourage them to connect with you on LinkedIn.

A word about business cards. Yes, they're old school, but they're still nice to have and they cost next to nothing. To be clear, I'm talking about personal cards you hand out when you're networking as yourself, not on behalf of your employer.

Most printing companies have online platforms that provide a variety of card templates for you to choose from and many allow you to custom design your card. In addition to providing your name and contact information, indicate how you're branding yourself. You might want to list your areas of expertise with a few bullet points or upload a photo to increase the likelihood of being remembered. I have a little box on my desk full of cards from people I've met, and seeing their faces helps me recall who they are. For brand consistency, use the same photo as your LinkedIn profile, which should exude a vibe that matches the branding statement you created in Chapter 3.

Be creative. Think about adding a quote, whether out of your mouth or someone else's, that communicates your *je ne sais quoi*. In one iteration of my comedy cards, I had a photo of myself with a Guinness in hand and the words "My favorite beer is my third" underneath. (I often fantasized about "accidentally" handing those out at a work-related function.) You can use the back of your card, too. Some people place a QR code on there to enable their information to be delivered electronically. Just make sure everything on your card, right down to your choice of fonts, aligns with your brand.

You don't want to feel obligated. If anyone is kind enough to share their insights and perhaps take action on your behalf, you do have to be a decent human being and maintain professionalism in return. I've seen a friendship disintegrate after a person facilitated the hiring of one of her contacts and then a couple of weeks later the guy quit for a better position with another company. If you're not comfortable having someone advocate for you because you'd feel terrible if it didn't work out, you can say, "I so appreciate your willingness to vouch for me, but I think I'm more comfortable going through the normal hiring channels. Who do you suggest I contact about this opportunity?"

Sometimes people can be *too* helpful, as when you ask a person how they got into their line of work and then they bombard you with a mass of information that's disproportionate to your level of interest. Instead of concluding, "Welp, I guess I'm gonna sell mortgages now…" tell the person, "You've certainly given me a lot to think about. As you know, this is a new direction for me, and I want to take some time to consider it fully before I move forward. I'll be sure to keep you posted. Thanks a million for your help."

You don't want to bother anybody. If someone asked you for your help, I bet you'd be happy to oblige. People are typically flattered to be asked to share their knowledge and they feel good when they can contribute to another person's success. You'll bother them only if you're a pain in their ass. Don't worry, if you're concerned about being a bother, you're self-aware enough that you won't be.

Why you want to network

To gather information. Reading about the medical coding profession is not the same as learning about it from someone who does it for a living. Networking allows you to get a real-world, insider's perspective of an industry, occupation, or a particular company's culture that you won't find on the Internet. Your contacts may offer ideas you haven't thought of or suggest something related to what you think you want to do but didn't know existed.

Through networking, you might learn of opportunities that have not yet been made public. Once a position is posted online your competition skyrockets, so being able to approach a company beforehand gives you a tremendous advantage. This is a win-win situation. Human resource personnel, recruiters, and hiring managers much prefer having people referred to them by someone they know and trust. That saves them from having to sift through hundreds of resumes from candidates who may or may not be qualified—or truly interested—in the position or the company.

To validate your intentions. If the information you collect confirms you're on the right path and your contact feels you'd be a good fit for what you're considering, you'll move forward with greater confidence. On the other hand, upon learning more, you may realize that the direction you're considering isn't for you at all. Better to wonder what the hell you were thinking sooner rather than later.

To create awareness. Sometimes you just want people to keep you in mind should they hear of employment opportunities you might be interested in or know of other individuals or resources that would be helpful to you. The more people who are keeping their eyes and ears open for you, the better.

Identify people who can help you

Who could be in your network? Anyone you know as well as people you know of but haven't actually met. Let's narrow that down. Create a spreadsheet and list the people who are most in a position to help you. Start with your tribe and then think of the friends, neighbors, and coworkers you've had over the years. Also think of the "high traffic" folks you know who come in contact with a ton of people in the course of a day—hairdressers, baristas, nail technicians, bartenders, grocery store cashiers.

What role might these people play in helping you get to where you want to be? Do they have specific information you'd like to know? Do you want to bounce ideas off them because you admire their judgment and open-minded way of thinking? Do you just want to make them aware of what you're planning to do?

Now determine the best way to communicate with each of them. What's the optimal method of outreach? Is it best to call the person, send an email, contact through social media, or wait until the next time you see them?

We've all heard the phrase "It's not what you know, it's who you know." Let's twist that around to "It's not who you know, it's who knows *you*." Who needs to know about you?

Let's say you met someone briefly in a social situation or you've been following a person you admire on social media. To get on their radar, find them on LinkedIn and send a message through that platform. (To send a message to someone you're not connected with, you may need to upgrade your account or take advantage of a free trial upgrade.) By reaching out this way, with just a click they can review your well-crafted LinkedIn profile. Once they see how amazing you are and how much passion you have for what you do, they'll be more excited to meet with you or help you out.

Set up and conduct a networking meeting

I think the best way to establish or strengthen a relationship is through a meeting, either in person or by teleconference. People get a million emails and phone calls. You'll make a greater impact if they can see your face.

Here's how to write an email or LinkedIn message asking for a brief meeting:

Reinforce your connection. As applicable, make it known up front if a mutual friend or colleague suggested you connect with them.

"Our mutual friend, Jen Blair, suggested I reach out to you."

Or remind them of how they know you.

"I enjoyed meeting you last week at the Chamber of Commerce presentation."

Maybe you have no connection, but the person is someone you want to make yourself known to. You might open with something like this:

"I've been following you here on LinkedIn and particularly enjoyed your article on…"

State your purpose for writing. In business writing you almost always want to state your purpose up front. This gives your reader a context in which to put the information that is to come.

"After fifteen years in B2B marketing, I'm exploring career opportunities in event planning. I've always been interested in that industry, and based on my research, the skills I've honed over the years should transfer well. Jen tells me you're the best out there, and I would so appreciate your insights as to how to break into this field."

Ask for a meeting.

"If possible, I'd love to get together for a brief meeting either in person or through video conferencing—whatever you prefer. I promise I won't take more than twenty minutes of your time. Please let me know what your schedule allows."

In future communication, let your contact decide when and the best way to meet. Make it clear that you're willing to travel to a location that's convenient for them, and if you do meet for coffee, of course you pick up the tab.

If you don't get a response after a couple of weeks, follow up. Just once, though. Keep in mind that some people are truly over-networked; everyone wants to pick their brain. No matter how much they sincerely would like to help you, they simply may not have the time. If they respond saying their schedule doesn't allow for a meeting, don't push the issue. Just say, "I understand. Thanks so much for getting back to me."

Conducting the meeting. Be sure to go into the meeting with a solid agenda; you have a lot of ground to cover in a limited timeframe. If you're exploring a new career path, you might ask these questions:

- How did you get started?
- What skills and personality characteristics are required to succeed in this line of work?
- What does a typical day look like for you?
- What is the most frustrating aspect of what you do?
- What advice would you give to someone starting out?
- What do you wish you'd known earlier about this line of work?
- Where do you see the industry going in the next few years?
- Can you recommend any resources I should look into or people I should try to connect with?

Do as much research as you can beforehand so your questions are more pointed. You don't want to take up someone's time if you haven't bothered to gain a basic understand of what you want to talk about. I enjoy helping new writers, and I enjoy helping them more when they've done some groundwork before approaching me. We won't get very far if they open the conversation with, "How do I write a memoir?" I'd be more impressed by "What are your recommendations for integrating backstory into a memoir?" That type of question indicates they've thought through their intentions.

Be respectful of your contact's time. Even if the meeting is going well and the person is clearly engaged and eager to help, at the fifteen-minute point, say, "I promised I would take only twenty minutes of your time, so I have just a couple of final questions." If they say don't worry about it, give it another fifteen minutes.

Wind it up by asking, "Now, what I can do for you?" Ideally, you'll be able to offer something in return, so during the course of the meeting, be on the lookout for how you might be of help to them.

After the meeting. Send the person an email or card thanking them for taking the time to meet with you. Unless you have an attachment or link to send, I think an old-fashioned thank you card sent via snail mail is a nice touch. I keep every thank you card I've ever received. Somehow indicate you've taken their advice—maybe you've ordered a book they recommended or initiated contact with a person they thought you should connect with.

Keep in touch periodically and be sure to let the person know when you've landed that next position. Tell them how valuable their insights and encouragement have been to you.

Every time you reach out to one of your contacts, record the date and nature of your interaction on your spreadsheet. Note important details of conversations you've had and whatever follow-up actions you need to take.

Expand your network—talk to strangers

Good luck often comes from strangers, so seize every opportunity to get yourself out in circulation. Nothing amazing is going to happen in your house; it's highly unlikely the Publisher's Clearinghouse van will be pulling up with a curbside delivery. When possible, take your laptop to your favorite coffeehouse or other public space and work on your stuff there. The energy in public places can be very inspiring, and no matter how shy you are, you're likely to meet somebody interesting. All you have to do is smile as people walk by. They might stop and ask what you're working on, and then you can say, "I'm looking for a job in…" or, "I'm defining my personal brand. How am I coming across to you?" That's how a conversation begins.

You never know who might be able to help you, but don't look at people only in terms of what they can do for you. Every contact you have with another human being is an opportunity to enrich somebody's life. Strike up a conversation while you're waiting in line at the grocery store or the post office. Just say something like, "How's your day going?" Offer a sincere compliment if you like their shoes or their purse or their hairstyle or their eyeglasses. You may be the only one who that person talks to all day.

I've met so many fabulous people at coffee shops and pubs and on airplanes. I've gotten freelance writing work from a substance abuse therapist I met in Starbucks and now Spero and I have been friends for years. I met my pal Warren on a Southwest flight from Albany to Las Vegas in 2011. We talked for five hours straight. He lives in Albany and has become a beloved member of our crazy clan, never missing a family birthday party or other gathering when I'm in town.

Warren is eighty-two years old now and is funny as hell. Whenever I need a laugh, I think of him telling this story about a visit to his local DMV. By some miracle, he was the only one in the place, so he bypassed the ropes and stanchions set up for crowd control and went straight to one of the reps behind the counter. The woman pointed to the non-existent queue and told him he had to go through the line properly. Though in disbelief, Warren obediently walked through the empty maze and stood there at the front. At that point, the woman looked up and said, "Next!"

If you meet only one stranger who has a story like that, it's all worth it.

Don't discount older people. Don't figure that just because someone appears to be retired they're out of circulation and are no longer relevant. That old guy you make eye contact with might own a company or have a family member who's doing exactly what you'd like to do. Or, like Warren, he may be one of the coolest people you've ever met.

I want to share two other encounters with strangers that affected my life in ways I'll never forget. The first occurred the day my father died of a massive heart attack. At the time, I was working for GE in Connecticut, and upon receiving the news, I sped up to Albany in a surreal fog. On my way to my sister's house, where everyone had gathered, I stopped at the bank to get some cash. This was before the ATM days, so I had to go inside. The teller, a young guy with "Chris" on his nameplate, performed the simple transaction as if I were the most valued customer who ever walked through the door. I'll never forget his smile; it was just what I needed.

"Thank you for being so nice to me," I told him. "I just found out my father died."

With that, he took my hand into both of his, looked me in the eye and said, "I'm very sorry to hear that." I was so touched by his kindness.

The second encounter is an example of attempting to practice what I preach about being nice to everyone. Coming out of CVS, I smiled broadly and held the door open for an elderly woman approaching the store.

"That's an exit!" she snapped, and then opened the door marked "Entrance" her own damn self. Made my freakin' day.

How to write a cover letter

Let's say you've heard about opportunities through your network or have found some positions online you'd like to apply for. Your resume is set to go, but *ugh!* Cover letters.

Do you absolutely need a cover letter? Yes. To me, sending a resume without a cover letter says you just couldn't be bothered. And if a posting specifically asks for a cover letter and you don't include one, they'll wonder what the hell is wrong with you that you can't follow simple directions.

One of my outplacement clients, who had been a hiring manager when his division closed, informed me with a certain degree of arrogance that he didn't need to write cover letters. Why? Because he never read them when he was assessing a candidate for a position. *Hmph.* I told him that's too bad, you can learn so much about a candidate from their cover letter. Beyond their command of grammar and usage and general ability to communicate in writing, a cover letter provides insight into a candidate's organizational skills, attention to detail, and personality.

Cover letters give you the opportunity to show why you're the perfect person for the job, the answer to their prayers. If your background is an obvious match for the position, you can keep your cover letter pretty simple and let your resume tell the story. Some situations, however, warrant some explanation. For example, if you're making a career change, you'll want to explain why you've decided to take a new direction and then highlight how your transferable skills could meet their needs.

Many clients have asked me to draft a "standard" cover letter for them. There's no such thing. There's no such thing as a one-size-fits-all cover letter that you can use for any old job you want to apply for. You may use parts of cover letters over and over, but always tailor each one to the position you're going for.

Here's the basic structure of a cover letter:

First paragraph. Let the reader know which position you're applying for and how you found out about it. If applicable, be sure to mention if a mutual contact has referred you to them or if you've already met somewhere.

Middle section. Specifically show how you meet their needs. Infer what some of their more important requirements are and show how you can handle them. It's okay to use bullets in this section, but don't lift the exact bullets from your resume. Paraphrase them a bit. Show passion for what you do—convey energy and enthusiasm.

Closing. Ask the reader to contact you for an interview. You can indicate you'll be calling to follow up, but these days that's almost impossible. You may have some luck if you're applying to a small company, although they also have protective gatekeepers.

Sample cover letters

Notice the difference in the two sample cover letters that follow. The first is in the "worth a try" category. It follows the structure I just gave you, but lacks the level of detail, company knowledge, and enthusiasm of the "hot prospect" letter that follows it.

> **Sample cover letter – "Worth a try"**
>
> Dear Hiring Manager:
>
> Please consider the attached resume for the Training Specialist position posted on your company's website.
>
> As you can see, I offer a solid background in both classroom and virtual training in a variety of industries including IT, health care, insurance, and financial services. With outstanding presentation skills and a down-to-earth personality that motivates participants to learn, I strive to deliver the curriculum in the most engaging manner possible. In addition to my training expertise, I am a skilled technical writer and can produce instructional materials of the highest quality.
>
> I am available immediately and can travel extensively—I love the road! If my background is of interest to you, please contact me at (702) 555-1111.
>
> I look forward to talking with you soon!
>
> Sincerely,

Sample targeted cover letter – "Hot prospect"

Greetings, ABC Company!

Please consider the attached resume in response to the Software Engineer position listed on your website.

I have been watching your company with a keen interest for several months and was impressed by your operational demo at the Tech Startup Showcase last weekend. I "get" what you do and can see the potential for explosive growth.

As a web developer, I have written large systems in Perl, PHP, JavaScript/jQuery, MySQL, and the supporting infrastructures for the printing, entertainment, and travel industries. Key projects include:

- A real-time event reservation engine adopted by multiple properties on the Las Vegas Strip. Project contributed over $1.5M to the company's bottom line through increased capability and expense savings.

- An automated system that creates and disseminates quotes for print products and facilitates payment, tracking, and reporting. Resulting process improvements save an estimated $25K per month.

- A web-based ordering portal that allows customers to order and track their customized print and promotional products. Project is currently in negotiation for sale to a major online retailer.

I would love to come in for an interview to show you some solutions I've crafted and explain how I could help your software extend its reach to other industries. I will call tomorrow to briefly introduce myself and to see if we can set a time to meet.

Thanks,

You may wonder whether the tone of the second letter is a bit too informal. Maybe it's fine for a start-up company with a youthful organizational culture, but it might not go over in a blue-chip conglomerate. Or would it? Maybe it would be different enough to get somebody's attention. Try not to go crazy second-guessing your approach, but as a rule, you're safer to error on the side of caution. In this case, the informal tone worked. The writer of that letter, which I modified to use as an example, was called for an interview the next day.

Cover letter Do's and Don'ts

Do:

- When sending an email, write your cover letter in the body of the email rather than attach it as a document. If the structure of an online application process requires you to upload a cover letter as an attachment, format it nicely as if you were dropping it in the mailbox.
- In the subject field of your email, indicate the position you're applying for and associated position number, if applicable.
- As with any type of business correspondence, make your cover letter *reader* focused, not *writer* focused. In other words, focus on their needs, not yours. Phrases such as "I am seeking…" and "This job would be perfect for my career development because…" are all about you. Your readers don't care why they're perfect for you; they want to know why you're perfect for them.
- Let your personality come through. Unlike your resume, which has no voice, your cover letter should sound like you, just as your LinkedIn profile summary should sound like you. People hire *people*. Don't be afraid to use exclamation points if you're an exclamation point type of person. They convey energy and enthusiasm. Don't overdo it, though. More than a couple might make you seem a little manic.
- Show you know something about the company. Have they been in the news lately? Do they have an exciting new product coming out? Are you a long-time customer? Do you admire their position in the industry?

- Mention compensation only if the posting asks for salary requirements. In that case, respond broadly. "My salary requirements are in the mid $70s, which based on my research, seems to be within the current market range for this type of position."
- Proofread your letter carefully. Read it aloud to hear how your message sounds. Your brain has a way of filling in words that aren't there and skipping over duplicate words, so read each word aloud again, this time with no attachment to their meaning. Human error is inevitable, and we've all found a typo a nanosecond after clicking Send. (I live in fear of what I might see after this book is in print.)
- Track your activity. Copy and paste the link to the job posting in a spreadsheet. Record the date of your outreach along with any subsequent interactions with company representatives. Capture important details. Don't delete opportunities that have hit the wall, either because they've sent you a rejection email or haven't gotten back to you. Instead, create a new page—I call it the dead zone— and move that information there. You'd be surprised how dead ends can sometimes come back to life.

Don't:

- Never open any business correspondence with "To whom it may concern" or "Dear Sir or Madam." If you know the name of the person you can say, "Dear Kristen Smith." Otherwise, "Dear Hiring Manager" or "Hello" are fine. In lieu of a salutation, you can also just say, "RE: Training Specialist #458910" and then get into the body of your correspondence. Always use a colon after a salutation in business writing; a comma is correct only for personal correspondence.
- Don't tell your reader what they already know. I've actually seen cover letters that say, "My resume will provide you with information concerning my abilities, employment history, and educational background." Call me crazy, but I'm guessing your reader is well aware of the purpose of a resume.

- Don't be presumptuous by saying something like, "I'm sure you will agree that my background is a perfect match for your qualifications." Let your readers draw their own conclusions.
- Even if you're open to a variety of different roles in a company, don't expect the reader to figure out your objective. "I would like to explore the possibility of joining your organization" says nothing. Specifically state the position or type of role for which you'd like to be considered.
- Don't include information that's not relevant to the position. Saying "I am open to extensive travel" means nothing if the posting makes no mention of travel at all.
- Don't highlight the fact that you lack one or more of the requirements stated in the job posting. Job postings are sometimes written hastily without much thought behind them or with an ideal candidate in mind who may or may not exist in real life. If you truly feel your background matches their needs, apply anyway. Just don't say, *"Although I lack experience in..."*
- On the other hand, I wouldn't bother applying for a position if you lack any of their "must have" requirements. They're stated as such for a reason.
- Don't start every sentence with "I." This is hard because after all, you're talking about yourself. Restructure sentences to get around that. For example, you could change "I have a background in..." to "My background encompasses..."

※

The amount of effort you put into a cover letter should be in proportion to your level of excitement about the position. As in sales, some prospects are hotter than others. You get psyched about opportunities that seem to be a perfect match for you and you look at others and think, *Meh, worth a try.*

Don't knock yourself out trying to write the perfect cover letter. As with your resume, it only has to be good enough. Overall, cover letters don't usually get a whole lot of attention, so don't fret too much about them. Still, do the best you can. As you're making yourself known to the world, your communication skills—

both verbal and written—are front and center. Maybe because I've been a writer for most of my life, I think it's important to be able to write well. Your writing represents you professionally. If you're a sloppy writer, your reader may wonder what other areas of incompetence lie under the surface.

Writing is hard. Writing well is even harder. This is something you might want to work on. I recommend starting with a little book, *Rewrite Right!* by Jan Venolia. Over the years, I've read many books on writing and this is the best I've come across to improve your basic writing skills. I understand that semicolons and active versus passive voice are not the most exciting topics, but you won't feel like you're in grammar hell. The information is presented in a simple way that is easily understood. This is a book you'll be happy to own.

Sadly, in the age of throwaway communication fueled by texting and careless posts on social media, the craft of writing seems to be deteriorating. Too many people don't write well enough themselves to assess the quality of someone else's writing. They can't distinguish well-crafted prose from a brain-dump stream of consciousness. But someday your writing will be in front of someone who does write well and who appreciates that you do, too. That person may have some influence on the direction of your life. Solid communication skills could weigh heavily on your being selected for a job, being offered a position at a higher salary, or being considered for a promotion. And the inability to write and speak well could cost you tens of thousands of dollars over the course of your career.

11. NAIL THE INTERVIEW

IF YOU HAVEN'T DONE A JOB SEARCH IN A WHILE, the thought of interviewing may feel overwhelming. This is the way I look at it:

> **An interview is nothing but a conversation between a couple of people who will someday be dead.**

What's the worst that can happen? Okay, my friend Linda in Australia once blew a snot bubble while laughing during an interview, but chances are you won't be doing that. In this chapter, I've asked some other friends to share their crazy experiences as well. Just keep in mind there's really nothing at stake. If you don't get the job, it's not the end of the world. Other jobs are out there.

We talked before about how a little stress can be good; it means we care. And while a certain amount of adrenaline keeps you sharp, too much can prevent you from functioning well. Have you ever been so stressed that your brain can't access something you absolutely know? That's because under pressure the prefrontal cortex, the part of your brain that controls thinking and reasoning, starts to shut down. To make sure that doesn't happen while you're interviewing, follow these three nuggets of advice:

Know your stuff. Review all the self-assessment exercises you did in the earlier chapters—the answers to many of the questions you'll be asked during the interview are right there in your own handwriting. Know the content of your resume frontwards, backwards, and inside out. ***Remember, the resume is not just your primary marketing tool, it's the focal point of the interview.*** I can't tell you how many times I've asked people about things I see on their resume only to hear, "I'm not sure what I had in mind when I put that down" or "I don't really know what that means. I got it off my job description." Be able to speak to everything on there and be sure to have the backstories fresh in your mind.

Love what you have to offer. Believe in your heart that a company should be praising Jesus to have you join them. You know exactly where you knock it out of the park, as well as all the other valuable skills you're bringing to the party, and you should have a burning desire to tell the world what you're all about.

Let you be you. Interviewers face an endless stream of candidates who are all trying hard to impress. After having met a multitude of people, do you think they're more likely to remember the person who answered every question mechanically by rote, or the person who provided meaningful human interaction, who wasn't continually pitching themselves, and actually made the conversation enjoyable?

You're not doing anyone a favor by putting on an Oscar-winning performance in the interview if you'll be stuck working in a place where you simply don't fit in. The further you are from the "real" you, the harder life becomes. Try to be the best version of yourself that you can keep up on a daily basis. Or even better, be the version of yourself that you like the most.

ೞҩ

Managing self-induced stress requires a good amount of preparation and the proper mindset. I'll be going over in detail how to nail that interview, but before we get into the nitty-gritty, let's talk about handling the initial call from a prospective employer or a recruiter working on an employer's behalf.

The initial call

You're in the drive-thru at Starbucks and a call comes in from a number you don't recognize. Don't answer; let it go to voicemail. Call the person back as soon as you're able to focus your attention, and when you do call back, expect anything. You could have a two-minute conversation with the sole purpose of setting up a time for an interview or the person could say, "Do you mind if I ask you a few questions?" and then launch into what turns out to be a half-hour screening interview. That's why you need to be prepared to perform in full interview mode at any time.

Have your resume, cover letter, and the job posting in front of you, but use them only as a crutch, and only if needed. Don't let them, or anything else, distract you from the conversation. We all know what it's like to talk to someone who's obviously multitasking. Annoying.

Phone communication poses challenges. Something like seventy percent of communication is nonverbal, and since you're not able to pick up on each other's visual cues, it's a little harder to build rapport. That makes it all the more important to convey enthusiasm and let them hear your smile in your voice.

When scheduling an interview, find out the name and the role of the person, or people, you'll be meeting with. Ask how much time you should allow, and if you'll be meeting onsite, block out a couple of hours beyond the time they give you. If you have a ten o'clock interview, don't go scheduling a lunch date at noon. They could run late, they may bring in other people to meet you, or they may have you take pre-employment assessments that you hadn't anticipated. You don't want to rush through an interview because you have to meet a friend at PF Chang's.

About panel interviews. If the person indicates you'll be having a panel interview with various members of the department, try to find out who will be there. You don't need to know their names at this point, just what their roles are so you can prepare to ask each person at least one question.

When the day comes, do get everyone's name, and preferably their business cards. That will make it easier to send a personalized thank you email. Write down their names according to how they're seated so you can use their names during the interview.

During a panel interview, make sure you make eye contact with everyone. It's easy to want to make eye contact with the nice person and avoid looking at the guy who gives a standoffish vibe. Make a conscious effort not to do that. Address whoever asked the question first and then look around to the rest of the people in the room.

You may feel a bit intimidated by a panel interview, more so than a one-on-one. As in comedy, never admit you're nervous. You don't want the people in front of you to look for signs of your anxiety when they should be paying attention to how you're answering their questions. Don't worry. You'll be well prepared, and you'll be fine.

Screening interviews

Screening interviews are usually conducted by someone from human resources or an internal or third-party recruiter contracted by a company to search for and evaluate candidates. The screener's objective is to confirm you have the basic skills the position requires, assess your communication skills, and determine whether you'd fit into the company's culture. Based on this initial meeting—which could be conducted on the phone, through a video conference, or in person—they'll decide whether you'll proceed to the next step in the selection process.

As to what that next step might be, again, expect anything. It could be a one-on-one interview with the hiring manager or a panel interview with the hiring manager and some team members. It could involve pre-employment testing to assess your job knowledge, skills, personality, or cognitive or physical abilities. With your permission, they may conduct a pre-employment background check. They might even have you do some kind of automated video interview with pre-set questions that you answer into the camera on your laptop, maybe without the opportunity for a do-over. Yep, you're looking in the camera, talking to nobody. Weird, I know. I've never done one of these, but I can imagine myself accidentally swearing and then spending the rest of the time apologizing and talking myself into a pitiful abyss.

It's possible that the first person you sit with could be the hiring manager. Since they know the ins and outs of the job more so than an HR rep or a recruiter, hiring managers look at you from a different perspective. They want to know 1) Do you have the skills and knowledge the position requires? 2) Will you fit in with their team? and 3) Do they like you enough to have you as a direct report? Hiring managers are likely to make the ultimate decision, but don't discount recruiters and

HR reps. Don't think you'll save "the good stuff" for the person who really matters. If you don't get past the screener, you're not going anywhere. For insight into a company's selection process, see what other candidates have said on Glassdoor.com and other online resources.

Remember how I told you to expect anything? Years ago, a third-party recruiter set me up for a telephone screening interview with a hiring manager and another writer in his department. We had a productive and fun conversation, and at the end the hiring manager told me I'd definitely be asked to come in for a face-to-face meeting in his office. About fifteen minutes later, the recruiter called me with an offer—her client wanted to hire me sight unseen. I thought that was pretty risky because God knows if I had to work side-by-side with someone every day, I'd want to make damn sure they didn't smell or have anything weird about them. It's unusual to be hired after just a telephone interview, but anything is possible. That turned out to be a great gig.

Working with third-party recruiters

Third-party recruiters and staffing agencies source and qualify candidates on behalf of their client companies who are seeking to fill permanent, temporary, and/or temp-to-perm positions. They charge their client companies a flat fee for each candidate placed or a fee based on the percentage of the salary for each placement. There should never be a cost to you. If anyone tries to charge you with the promise of placing you in a position, run!

Some people are reluctant to work with recruiters because they think the recruiter's fees come out of the salary they'd be getting, and they'd be better off applying to the company directly. That's not the case. Recruiters earn their fees by doing all the legwork so they can present their clients with only the top candidates. If companies had to do the sourcing and preliminary screening themselves, they would still incur the expense of the internal resources required to do that.

Good recruiters will give you objective feedback on your resume, will let you know what they think your chances are of landing the type of position you're looking for, and they'll tell you whether or not your salary expectations are realistic. They know their clients well, and with an inside view of a company's culture and the preferences of the individuals with hiring authority, they can coach you on how to best respond to interview questions. Generally, recruiters will share the feedback they received from the client company on how you did. They often serve as a mediator in salary negotiations, although it's not the recruiter's job to negotiate the final offer or ensure you get the best deal.

Recruiters will want to know the details of your search to date—where you've applied, where you've interviewed, and what your salary requirements are. They won't present you to a client if you're looking for compensation beyond the range established for the position or if you've already approached the company on your own. This is because many clients will nullify your candidacy in the case of a duplicate submission. Always be direct with recruiters; if you betray their trust up front, it's game over.

As a job seeker, I've had many positive experiences with third-party recruiting firms. I've also applied to positions posted by recruiters and never heard back. My impression is that recruiters are hot for you only if your resume hits their desk when they have a matching position to fill or if your skillset fulfills an ongoing need. Don't expect recruiters to proactively market you or keep you in mind should a position matching your background surface in the future, although I know some who do just that. I've had inquiries from recruiters years after my initial outreach.

For sure, some recruiters are better than others. As with resume writers, anyone can call themselves a recruiter, so do your due diligence. Unless someone has personally referred you to a third-party recruiter who works independently, you may feel more comfortable with one who's affiliated with an established firm. It's okay to work with more than one recruiter, but do let them know that the relationship is not exclusive.

It's important to understand that recruiters work on behalf of their client company, not the job seeker. That said, it's in their best interest to ensure you're a good fit for the job and will have a positive employment experience. They want your placement to be a long-term success as much as you do.

Addressing salary early on

The screener may ask about your salary expectations, and that's fair enough. Salaries for some professions can range broadly, and if you're at a level that's twenty thousand dollars more than what the company is prepared to offer, there's no point in moving the conversation forward. This saves time for all parties involved.

You need to have a well thought out strategy to address salary and to be able to deliver it with confidence. Before you even send out a resume, have a dollar figure in mind that you absolutely *must* make in order to meet your monthly living expenses. The math has to work out or you'll need to find an additional source of income to make up for the shortfall. This rock-bottom salary figure would be something to consider only if everything else about the job is ideal, and I mean *everything*. I'd work for next to nothing to be Bill Murray's personal assistant, but for jobs based in reality, I wouldn't want to sell myself short.

If a screener asks for your salary expectations, say something like, "Once I have a clearer understanding of the scope of responsibilities, I'll be in a better position to discuss salary. But based on my research, it seems a role like this might pay in the [give a salary range]. Is that in your ballpark?"

How they respond is very telling. If they say, "Yes, that's definitely in our range," you probably have some room to negotiate down the line. If you sense some hesitancy, make a mental note that you may have to create a strategy to justify your expectations. Not now, though. **You can't negotiate salary until you're offered the position.** Once you get an offer, you'll want to know every detail about the total compensation package. At this point, however, it's too early in the process to go any deeper than to give a broad range. You can close the topic by saying, "I'm sure if we both feel good about how I fit into the position, then salary won't be an issue."

I generally don't recommend bringing up salary or benefits or anything related to *your* needs. At this point, it's all about *their* needs. It's possible to go through one or more interviews and still not know what the compensation package looks like. That's okay; the more you learn about the responsibilities and demands of the position, the better you'll be able to determine what a fair salary would be.

In the beginning of your search, take every interview you can. The more interviewing experience you get, the better you'll be at it and the more confidence you'll develop. It's like the comedy mantra, "Stage time, stage time, stage time." And keep in mind that once you get in front of someone and they see how awesome you are, they may be so impressed that they'll consider you for a different, higher paying role in their organization. Or they may even create a position for you. Anything is possible.

That said, you may reach a point where you no longer need the interviewing practice and you don't want to bother getting all dolled up and schlep across town for a job with a salary that turns out to be nowhere near what you're willing to take. In that case, it's fine to say, "Before we go any further, I'd hate to take up your time if we're not on the same page regarding salary. Can you give me an idea of the range you're offering for this position?"

Whatever you do, if you hear a figure that's below your expectations, don't make the mistake of asking, "Is that negotiable?" You can't negotiate salary until you have an offer, but never ask that question even after you get an offer. Banish those words from your vocabulary. The person could respond with a simple, "No, it's not," and then you've driven yourself to a dead end.

When asked about your salary expectations, never respond with, "Well, I'm currently making…" You may currently be making much less than what the market pays for that type of position, and by coming in low, you could cheat yourself out of a higher salary that they might have been perfectly willing to pay. If your present company pays more than the going market rate, you could price yourself out of competition. And if you're changing careers, you'll likely be comparing apples and oranges.

You deserve a fair salary based on the scope of responsibilities, the level of skill required, and what the market pays in your geographic area. What you need to live on and what you're currently making do not factor into that equation.

Interviewing – Before

The better prepared you are, the more confident you'll be going into an interview. Here's what to do beforehand to ensure you present yourself in the best light possible.

Research the company

You're sure to be asked what you know about the company, and you'll need to know more than the fact that they have a job opening that interests you. Start your research by reviewing every page of their website. You can sometimes get a sense of a company's culture by the content and/or the tone of what's on there, and if you're lucky, they'll tell you what they actually do. I'm shocked by how often I see nothing but jargony corporate-speak about "mission-critical engaging" and "creating synergies" and "galvanizing in the face of perpetually changing technological landscapes." I want to scream, "BUT WHAT THE F**K DO YOU DO?!" That's a huge fail. If they're big enough to have a Wikipedia page, that might give you more straightforward information.

Google the company to see how they've been reported in the media. Read online reviews from consumers and check Glassdoor.com to see what former employees have to say. Peruse their social media. Summarize what you've learned in a couple of sentences. You'll need this later.

Research the interviewer

Know who you'll be meeting with. Review the person's LinkedIn profile and look for things you have in common. Maybe you graduated from the same school, follow the same thought leaders, or support the same non-profits. Make a mental note in case this seems natural to bring up during the interview.

I could tell you to keep it on a professional level and don't be a creeper peering into their personal life, but they're probably peering into yours, so go for it if you want. Just don't say, "I see on Facebook that you've been married to your wife, Jen, for twelve years and have two boys, ages seven and ten. Has your dad recovered from that pneumonia?" That would be hilarious, but not what I would recommend.

Know what you're going to wear

Fortunately, thanks to teleconferencing and a more relaxed workplace, the days of having to interview in an Easter suit are pretty much a thing of the past. If you own a suit and want to wear it, fine. A suit makes an awesome impression. It's possible to overdress for an interview, but that's not likely, and it's better to err on the side of being more formal than less. A good rule is to dress for the role you're going for and then click it up a couple of notches.

Some companies are known for their casual work environments, where flip flops and pajama bottoms are the norm. Don't think it's okay to dress down to match their company culture—you're not part of their culture yet. You're an outsider coming in for a business meeting. Look the part.

I wouldn't get too caught up trying to figure out what "power colors" you should wear. If you want to convey authority, there's nothing like a suit or a dark blazer. I feel it's most important to choose something that you feel good in and that exudes your personal brand. By now your closet should be filled only with clothes that bring you joy, so that shouldn't be hard.

Whatever you plan to wear, make sure you inspect it and try it on well beforehand. The morning of the interview is not the time to discover a stain on your lapel or that you've put on ten pounds since your cousin's wedding two summers ago. Make sure you're comfortable walking, standing, and sitting. You can't answer questions intelligently when your waistband is cutting off circulation to your brain.

> *"I had breast reconstruction surgery and decided to go way bigger than my old set. A few months afterward, I had an interview and wore my 'I always get the job in this' suit. When I sat down with the interviewer, the top button popped off. Oops!"*
> *– Carrie S.*

You may be tempted to capitalize on God's gifts to get what you want, but short skirts and low-cut tops are not the way to go (although Las Vegas does have its own set of rules). Stay away from open-toe shoes and stripper heels. Don't wear jewelry that clinks every time you move. And the world will thank you for not overdoing the cologne or perfume. In fact, better to forgo scents altogether since many people have allergies and other sensitivities.

The interviewer assumes this is the best you're ever gonna get, so take a good look in the mirror. How can you spruce yourself up? Do you need a haircut? A root job? Cooler looking eyeglasses? During an in-person interview your hands are visible to others, so make sure your nails are well groomed. That goes for guys, too. I could gag just by thinking of men with long or gnarly fingernails. Regardless of their competency, that would be a deal breaker for me. No way could I be around that every day.

> *"I once interviewed a guy who had an obscenity tattooed on his forearm. I asked him about it, and the interview ended there. He came back three weeks later, after having spent three hundred dollars to obscure the message. I gave him the job. I feel like I changed his life a little." – Lori B.*

Know where you're going

Running late will cause your stress level to soar, so take every precaution to prevent that from happening. If applicable and feasible, take a test run at the same time of day as your interview to get a sense of the traffic situation. On the day of the interview, give yourself an additional fifteen minutes of travel time as a cushion. Despite your best efforts, some things are truly beyond your control, so don't freak if there's an unexpected backup or accident. And don't rush—bad things can happen when you're in a hurry. Call and give a heads up that you'll be a few minutes late. Chance are they'll understand, and if they don't, you probably wouldn't want to work for them anyway.

Gather your support materials

Take all this with you to an onsite interview or have this in front of you during a phone or virtual interview:

- A few copies of your resume
- Your list of references (I'll talk about references soon)
- A printout of the job posting
- A printout of some information about the company
- Your list of questions to ask
- Your answers to anticipated questions
- Samples of your work
- A few of your personal business cards
- Contact information for the person you'll be meeting with

I can't stress enough the importance of taking a few copies of your resume with you to an onsite interview. If for some reason the person can't find your resume and you don't have extras on hand, how is that interview going to proceed? Take several copies so you can whip them out if they bring other people in to meet you.

Buy or borrow a nice leather (or fake leather) portfolio to contain this stuff. Many come with a pad of paper and a place for a pen, which comes in handy for taking notes. While it's okay to record details you want to be sure to capture correctly, such as the name of a website the interviewer mentions or information regarding benefits, you break eye contact when taking notes so don't overdo it.

Prepare a list of questions to ask

Think of the interview as a conversation, not an interrogation. Don't make the mistake of allowing a structure where they ask you a question, you answer, they ask you another question, you answer, and so on until they say, "So, do you have any questions?" Feel free to ask questions as they come to you, as long as they relate to the topic at hand.

The question to ask ASAP

There's one question you want to weave into the conversation as soon as you can, and it goes something like this:

What do you feel are the most important skills or other qualities needed to succeed in this position?

The answer reveals what they believe their ideal candidate looks like. Find this out early on—this information will help you answer questions that are to come.

For example, when they ask, "What are your strengths and weaknesses?" you're going to present the strengths in your skill set that *they just told you* are the most important to succeed in that job. Keep their idea of success in mind throughout the interview.

If you don't ask this, you'll be answering their questions based on what you've inferred from the job posting, which may or not be an accurate representation of what they actually want. Better to ask than to march down a path of false assumptions until you realize, *Oh, THAT'S what they're looking for…*

So how do you weave in this question without appearing pushy or as if you're trying to take control of the meeting? As soon as it seems natural, after you've answered one of their questions, tack this question on to the end of your answer while you have the stage. You can use this technique throughout the interview to maintain a conversational structure.

Other questions you might want to ask

Not every one of the following questions will be applicable to your situation. Depending on your priorities, you'll want to inquire about other considerations such as travel requirements, the option to telecommute, or opportunities for overtime.

- **Beyond the job description, what would you love to see the person in this position accomplish?**

    This question shows you're forward-thinking and are willing to go above and beyond.

- **How long have you and the rest of the team worked here?**

    This will give you an idea of their turnover. A lot of turnover is never a good sign.

- **Why is this position open?**

    You want to know if this is a new position or if the person who previously held it was promoted or jumped out a window because they couldn't stand the stress.

- **What do you like most about working here?**

    I would interpret any hesitation or lack of enthusiasm in their response as a red flag.

- **Does this position report to you?**

    You may hit it off with the interviewer, but if you'd be a direct report to someone else, you definitely want to meet that person before accepting the job since the person you report to can make or break your happiness at work.

- **How would you describe your management style?**

    Don't be afraid to ask this—a secure leader will be happy to talk about their management style. But don't take their words at face value; watch their body language, too.

- **What is the typical career progression for someone in this position?**

    Note how well the projected career path aligns with your expectations.

- **How do you see this role evolving?**

  The answer will tell you whether their plans for the position are aligned with what you want to do.

- **What direction would you love to see this department, or the company as a whole, take in the next few years?**

  As with the two previous questions, you'll gain some understanding of the potential for growth. You'll also get an idea of the interviewer's sense of vision.

- **Are there training opportunities for professional growth?**

  If so, this indicates the company invests in its employees and probably promotes from within. By asking this question, you show you're eager to gain new skills and further develop those you already have.

- **Realistically, how many hours a week does it take to do this job well?**

  This one is risky since you don't want to come across as a clock watcher. But if your priorities and values would be compromised by being tied to your laptop on nights and weekends, then you won't be happy in a job where you're expected to do just that. You could add, "While I'm certainly willing to work above and beyond as needed, I wouldn't be able to accept a position that requires a fifty-hour work week as a way of life." If it's game over, so be it. Better to know up front. Unless you want your job to consume your entire life, my advice is never work for a workaholic. And if they say, "I'm a workaholic, but I don't expect you to be," they're lying. Personally, I'd rather work for an alcoholic than a workaholic. I've worked for both, and believe me, the alcoholic was a lot easier to deal with and was infinitely more entertaining.

- **What are your immediate priorities for the next person who holds this position?**

  If they rattle off a whole list of things that need immediate attention, chances are you'll be walking into a mess. I'd be concerned as to why. While this could give you the opportunity to improve processes and put a feather in your cap, it could also mean the scope of the job is wider than you thought. Keep that in mind in case you get an offer and need to develop your negotiating strategy.

- **What does a typical day look like for the person in this role?**

  You'll not only get an idea of what the job is like, but just how familiar the interviewer is with the position.

- **What do you feel are the biggest challenges facing someone in this position?**

  This is a nice way of asking, "What could potentially suck about this job?"

- **Tell me about the responsibilities that aren't listed in the job posting.**

  In other words, what lies behind "other duties as required"?

- **How would you describe the organizational culture here?**

  By the time you ask this question, you'll have already formed some impression of the culture. If it doesn't match what the interviewer tells you, be on the lookout for other things that don't seem to add up. Note how well their culture aligns with the Likes and Dislikes you identified in Chapter 4.

- **How is success measured?**

  This question shows you intend to do well and exceed their performance expectations.

- **How will I know whether or not I'm doing a good job?**

  The answer will give you some idea of their communication style and how they give feedback.

Prepare answers to questions you might be asked

Expect to be asked a combination of traditional interview questions and behavior-based questions. Behavior-based questions often begin with "Tell me about a time when…" or "Give me an example of how you…" They're based on the logic that how you've handled situations in the past is indicative of what you can do in the future. Don't worry about which category the questions fall into, just make sure you can answer them.

Having already done such great self-assessment work, the answers to many of the interviewer's questions will come to you easily. But not all will. Be careful; assume that everything you say can and will be used against you, so say what you mean and mean what you say.

I strongly suggest you write out the answers to what you feel are the toughest questions beforehand.

If a response doesn't immediately come to mind as you read through these questions right now, what will come out of your mouth during the interview? The process of writing forces you to organize and articulate what you want to say and will prevent you from rambling like an idiot. I can't stress this enough. After you've written your answers, read them over and over. Don't memorize them to recite back; internalize them and *believe* them so you can speak with confidence.

Here are some questions you should be prepared to answer:

- **Tell me about yourself.**

    This is a typical ice breaker, and it's easy to mess up because it's so open ended. Since it's probably going to be the first thing you say of substance, you need to nail this. Interviewers form an impression of you within the first couple of minutes and the rest of the time they're deciding whether or not their impression was correct. I recommend this approach:

How to answer "Tell me about yourself"

1. Say where you're from, especially if you're in a transient city such as Las Vegas. People are curious.
2. Present a brief overview of your background in chronological order (unlike your resume, which presents your experience in reverse). Pepper this with words of enthusiasm and self-assurance such as "I loved…" or "I realized I was good at…"
3. Explain why you're applying for this position. Nip that topic right in the bud.
4. Conclude with "And that's what brings me here today." This provides a nice segue that indicates you're ready to proceed with the interview.

For example, let's say I've had enough of career development and I've decided to pursue an opportunity in sales. My "Tell me about yourself" response would look something like this:

"Tell me about yourself" – Linda's example

"I'm originally from upstate New York, where I began my career. Through most of the 90s I facilitated career transition workshops for a company that, at the time, was the largest outplacement firm in the world. After I moved out West, I worked on some interesting contract assignments in corporate training and technical writing.

"In 2013, I was happy to return to career development, which I've always loved. In addition to consulting with clients, I managed operations of the Las Vegas office, and a part of my job was business development. I found I enjoyed the challenge of bringing in new corporate clients, and during my tenure in the position, the business grew by more than fifty percent.

"Having worked for so many years in career services, I'm ready for a change. Given my success in sales, it seems like a natural transition, and that's what brings me here today."

Don't get too long-winded with this or any other question you're asked. Prepare your response so you can deliver it in about a minute. If you're rattling on longer than that, the interviewer is probably itching to get on to the next question.

You don't need to get into anything personal here. The fact that you're a proud parent of two beautiful daughters and that you've an avid hiker is awesome, but rarely plays into this scenario.

- **What did you like, and not like, about your last (or current) job?**

  Easy enough. Refer back to your Likes and Dislikes exercise. Choose a couple of Likes that you anticipate being conditions of the job you're going for and one Dislike that is not.

  "I loved helping people with financial planning and researching the options that are best for their needs, which is why this position excites me. On the downside, the commute was brutal, so I'm thrilled that your office is so close to my house."

  You can also choose a Dislike that you really never want to do again.

  "Although I've been told I'm a strong leader, I don't enjoy having direct reports. I much prefer being an individual contributor, which is one of the reasons why I find this position so appealing."

- **What do you know about our company?**

  You'll have done your research, but don't feel you have to report back everything you've learned.

  "I've done some research and was surprised to see that your organization dates back to 1964. Your consumer reviews are consistently positive, which says a lot about your commitment to quality. How do you think your plans to expand into new markets will affect the responsibilities of this position?"

  Note how I tacked on a related question at the end.

- **Where do you see yourself five years from now?**

Ugh, who doesn't dread this question? Though your knee-jerk reaction might be to offer some kind of glib response, squash that temptation. Interviewers have heard it all, and they won't be amused. There's a place for humor during the interview, which I'll get into later, but trying to be clever in lieu of answering a question is never cool.

Interviewers ask this to see how long you intend to stay with their company and whether or not your career goals align with the company's needs. That's fair enough; filling positions and onboarding new employees requires considerable time, effort, and money. They want to make sure their investment in you will be worth it.

This is probably the only question where offering a general answer is better than being specific. Rather than specifying a particular position you'd like to assume up the ladder, give the impression that you'd be content growing in the role you're interviewing for.

"That's a tough question considering how things change so rapidly. Right now, I see myself continuing to lead interesting projects and adding to my skill set so I can take on greater responsibilities in this role and support the company's growth."

I know that sounds bullshitty, but this is one of those questions where you just have to play the game. It's not like you have a crystal ball, right?

If I were interviewing for a position as a career specialist, I would say something like this:

"Whether five, ten, or twenty years from now, I expect to be continuing to help people find work that brings them joy. That's where my passion lies, and I don't see that changing anytime soon."

No bullshit there. Plus, by projecting so many years into the future, I put the kibosh on any concerns they may have that I might retire soon.

Never let it slip that you eventually intend to move on to a sexier company, and keep any aspirations for going back to school, starting your own business, or retiring on a beach in Mexico to yourself. Answer as if you intend to work there forever. If this seems a little untruthful, think about the question they're asking you. What company can tell you with a straight face that they can guarantee the position you're interviewing for—or even the company itself—will even exist in five years?

- **What are your strengths and weaknesses?**

You know what your strengths are. And earlier in the interview, you asked about the most important skills needed to succeed in the position. Present two or three of your strengths that match their picture of success.

As for weaknesses, don't offer the clichéd, "I'm such a perfectionist; I just want everything to be done well." Present a true weakness—just one—but something that wouldn't be a deal breaker. I would never admit (except to you) that people who talk too much bug the living shit out of me or that my Seven Dwarfs name would be Bossy. Indicate that it's something you're working on.

"Like many people, speaking to large groups does not come easily to me. I've found some good YouTube videos and I'm looking into joining one of the local Toastmaster chapters to help me gain some confidence in that area."

Of course, that won't work if public speaking is a skill that's critical to your success in the job. Choose a weakness that's not likely to be at all related to the job you're going for. You could say you're not good with numbers, but only if you're positive that the job requires zero math skills. Or choose a weakness related to something you never want to do again and you wouldn't take a job that required it.

- **Why should we hire you?**

Answer this by showing how you meet their needs and how you'd fit into their culture.

"Based on what I've learned about the goals for the position and for your company, I'm confident I have the know-how and drive to get things done. I've managed many large-scale projects in this industry, and almost all were delivered on time and within budget. Plus, I'm a good person to work with. I'm helpful to my coworkers and they know they can count on me."

Other questions you should be prepared to address
<ul><li>How would your colleagues describe you?</li><li>What makes you unique? What can you do that other candidates are not likely to do?</li><li>Why do you want to work here?</li><li>What are you most proud of in your career?</li><li>What would you do differently?</li><li>Tell me about a time when your work was criticized.</li><li>How have you handled disagreements with management or coworkers?</li><li>How do you provide constructive feedback?</li><li>Give me an example of how you motivate employees or coworkers.</li></ul>

When it comes to answering questions during the interview, it's best to play it safe, especially if you really need the job. That said, the more your responses are aligned with your personal truth, the better you'll fit into their organization. You'll have given them a clear idea of what they'd be getting, and they wouldn't ask you to join them if they weren't cool with that. The downside is, your personal truth is not always what they want to hear, which could reduce the likelihood of getting an offer. No matter what, present the truth in the most diplomatic way you can.

Prepare a list of references

Although the practice may seem a bit outdated, many companies still check references as a way to verify what you've shared in the interview and to learn more about what you're like to work with.

Identify individuals who can best vouch for the skills required for the position you're going for (relevancy is important) and who can attest to your ability to play nicely in the workplace. Consider supervisors, coworkers, colleagues, vendors, customers, mentors, and board members. They are likely to be the same people who would write a recommendation for your LinkedIn profile, so there's a good chance you've already been in touch with them. An upcoming interview gives you the opportunity to touch base again, and if you haven't already, ask if they're comfortable serving as a reference.

Using the same format as your resume with all your contact information at the top, create a separate document with the heading "References." Five references are ideal; come up with three as a minimum. For each person, list the following:

- Their name
- Their current title and company
- Their preferred email address and phone number
- A brief statement describing your relationship ("Reported directly to Tom for three years at ABC Industries.")

Years ago, companies would ask for both business references and personal references, meaning people outside of the work environment who can speak about your character and integrity. I don't hear of personal references being asked for much anymore, but anything's possible. Unless they specifically ask for personal references, or if you're early in your career and that's all you have, include only work-related references on your list.

Preparing for a virtual interview

Virtual interviews are awesome in that you can do them in the comfort of your home, and you don't even have to wear pants. I still would, just in case you have to get up for some reason. (Although my friend Dave had his LinkedIn headshot taken in his underwear and he swears that's why his photo perfectly captures his persona.) On the downside, a weak connection, poor quality camera or microphone, or user error can be a major bummer. The last thing you want is to mess around with tech issues as you're trying to make a good impression. Here are some tips to help:

Do a test run. Ask a friend to meet with you using the same videoconferencing technology you'll be using on the interview. Make sure your speakers and mic are turned on and check the camera quality. The quality of your audio is much more important than video, but you still want to project a clear and detailed image of your face. Lighting makes a huge difference, and the best scenario is natural lighting that hits you directly. Do your test run at the same time of day as your interview so you know what the natural lighting will be like. If your connection is spotty, try moving closer to your wireless router.

Setup and background. Ideally, you want to set yourself up in a room that is private, quiet, and free from interruptions from kids and pets. If you're interviewing for a remote position or would sometimes like to work at home, show them your home office; don't set yourself up in the kitchen. Make sure the background is tidy, and don't have a toilet visible behind you (as my mother pointed out to me during a FaceTime call) or a plant that looks like it's growing out of your head. I don't love virtual backgrounds—I always wonder what people are hiding. Don't sit too close or too far from the screen and elevate your device so the camera is a little higher than eye level. You'll look better without a double chin.

Dress for the camera. Although you and I know pants are optional, it's probably a better idea to dress as you would for an in-person interview. There's a psychological impact of wearing interview attire, and you don't want to be *too* relaxed. I wouldn't worry about what the best colors for the camera are, just don't wear a busy print that might be visually overwhelming. As with an in-person interview, keep your jewelry simple. You don't want to be clinking away as you're talking.

Record a practice interview. Give your friend a list of questions to ask you and record the session so you can see how you're coming across on camera. Almost everyone has something weird that happens when they're nervous. Be on the lookout for verbal tics such as "like," "um," and "you know." Also notice if you're constantly playing with your hair or making some other distracting gesture.

Interviewing – During

Upon arriving (face-to-face interview)

As I mentioned before, plan on getting to the interview early, and allow for a cushion of time in case traffic is heavy. Enter the building about ten minutes before your appointment, no sooner. If you're there super early, sit in your car and review your resume and whatever else you feel you need to look at one last time.

Turn off your phone before you go in. Power it down; don't just put it on vibrate. That buzz-buzz-buzzing is just as distracting as an ill-timed "Werewolves of London" ringtone (although that could endear you to a Warren Zevon fan like me).

As you sit in the reception area, check out your surroundings and assess the vibe of the place. Notice what people are wearing and how they speak to each other. Do they look friendly and happy, or do they seem strung out? I don't have to tell you to be nice to the person out front. You'd be surprised how many hiring managers ask reception personnel for their impression of candidates, and trust me, their opinions weigh heavily.

When the interviewer comes to greet you, don't grunt as you heave yourself out of the cushy chair in the waiting area. Spring out of that thing, and as they lead you to the room where the interview will take place, don't be lagging ten feet behind. You'll have a hard time convincing anyone of your ability to work in a fast-paced environment if you can't keep up with a person walking down a hallway.

If the meeting is being held in their office, glance around and note things you might have in common. *Was that photo taken in Dublin? Isn't it fabulous?* Like attracts like, but keep it authentic. You can't go raving about Dublin if you've never been there. Don't be the Eddie Haskell of interview small talk.

Chapter 11. Nail the Interview

Here's an interesting start to an interview:

> *"I'm eighteen interviewing for my first full-time job. I'm a new father and I really need it. The interviewer comes in and introduces himself. As he goes to sit down, he completely misses his chair and as he falls on the floor, he throws his coffee cup against the wall. It smashes all over the place. I have a tendency to laugh at people being awkward, so I'm biting my tongue. As he pulled himself up, all I could see was his hand and then his eyes, and then he said, 'We should get started.' I got the job and then laughed my ass off in the car on the way home."*
> *– Comedian Steve McInelly*

Sit still, sit up straight, and look them in the eye

Fidgeting signifies a lack of control, and it drives people nuts. Guys, calm that jiggly leg. Ladies, stop playing with your hair and jewelry, and don't dangle your shoe off your toe; I happen to know there's no graceful way to retrieve it after it falls to the middle of the floor. Remind yourself to relax your hands and face; doing that will relax the rest of your body as well. (Practice that the next time at the dentist when you catch yourself clinging to the chair for dear life.) And of course, don't forget to sit up straight, with shoulders back and down. Maintain an open and relaxed posture. Don't cross your arms or sit on the edge of your seat.

Make eye contact, but don't think about it or you'll weird yourself out. Just be a normal person. And hope that the interviewer is normal, too. Sometimes they're not.

> *"Weird job interview—the entire time, the owner never looked me in the eyes. She looked my resume, the clock, her shoes. I got the job and had to leave after three months. Lesson learned: If someone cannot establish eye contact in a business or personal relationship, run the other way. Lack of eye contact is now a big red flag for me."* – *Prudence T.*

Just answer the damn question

I once asked a client, "When did you move to Las Vegas?" and I swear on a stack of *People* magazines he began his response with, "Well, my wife had a hysterectomy in 2006..." My eyes rolled back to my cerebellum, which is probably why I've been told I should never play poker.

Listen to the question and answer it. If you think a long and detailed backstory is going to lead to a riveting conclusion, I have news for you. At about the sixty-second mark, the listener's mind begins to wander and they're thinking about the next question they want to ask or what they're gonna have for dinner tonight. If you're going on any longer than that, they're jonesing to get rid of you.

Okay, maybe a "Tell me about a time when..." behavior-type question might require a few seconds more than a minute. But just a few. I can't be the only one who has zero tolerance for a Chatty Cathy. What you perceive as a charming gift of gab could knock you out of the running.

If you don't have an answer

No matter how prepared you are, sometimes you're asked a question and you ain't got nothin'. Don't repeat the question back to the interviewer—that's an obvious clue that you're stalling for time. Stay calm, take a deep breath, and don't start making shit up. There's nothing wrong with saying, "I can't think of an answer right now. I'm sure it will come to me when I get in the car."

If you think your answer sucked

Don't worry. If a better answer comes to you later in the conversation, just say, "Can we go back to your question about (whatever)? I'd like to clarify..." Chances are, however sucky you think your answer is, it won't be as bad as this one, which in the end happened to work out just fine.

> *"When I interviewed for the job I'm at now, the first question was, 'What is your idea of good customer service?' Without missing a beat, I replied, 'Number one, don't be a prick.' As the words came out of my mouth, I couldn't believe I was saying that. Much later, she told me that opening line sealed my being hired."*
> – Comedian Kenneth K. (Kento)

If you think they hate you

I know we're all the center of our own universe, but whatever negative vibes you think you're picking up might not have anything to do with you. We tend to put interviewers on a pedestal as if they're all-knowing and have the power to control our destiny, but they're just regular people. Like anyone else, they could be having an off day caused by any number of things… a warning light on their car dashboard, a spat with their partner over breakfast, or an elderly father who's taken to walking the neighborhood in his pajamas. You don't know what could be going on. Maybe the person on the other side of the desk doesn't like interviewing or feels they suck at it or maybe you're the first candidate they've ever had to interview and they're more uncomfortable than you are. If you feel the interviewer seems distracted or a bit off, don't try harder to sell yourself; make an extra effort to be kind.

Of course, there are idiots in all walks of life, and sometimes they're participating in the selection process. One time I was delivering a mock training as part of a panel interview and one of the members of the training team played on his cell phone during my entire presentation. Being easily annoyed as I am, I wanted to knock that goddamn phone out of his pasty little baby hands. If someone is downright rude or inappropriate, remind yourself that you're not there to take abuse. You always have the option to say, "You know, I don't think we're on the same page, and I'd hate to take any more of your time. I do appreciate your willingness to meet with me, and I hope you find someone who's a better fit for what you're looking for." Then gather your stuff and run.

> *"I had an interviewer read my palm. I didn't get the job. She never told me what she saw. I guess it wasn't good."*
> *– Author Rekaya Gibson*

If you truly think you're bombing

A comedian who bombs could be remembered for years. My mother still talks about how she and my father walked out of a George Carlin show because he was so terrible. *George freakin' Carlin.* More than three decades ago! Fortunately, a bombed interview will be forgotten in no time. Let it go, it's not the end of the world. Nobody expects perfection (nobody you'd want to work for, anyway) and chances are you didn't do as poorly as you think.

I understand how an experience like that can feel devastating—I've done comedy sets I still cringe over. I've learned that if I'm having an off night on stage, rather than give up and half-heartedly trudge through my set, I try to deliver my material as if I'm performing at Carnegie Hall and the audience is going bonkers for me. I plow through it. As uncomfortable as it is, an off night trains me to be a better performer. If you sense things are starting to go south during the interview, continue to give them your A-game. Act as if they're hanging onto your every word. Ignore the dipshit playing on his phone. You'll be stronger for it.

> *"The interviewers left the room for a minute to talk. I was sure I wasn't going to get the job, so I started spinning around in my chair and didn't stop until they came back, at which point I asked what the record was for the most spins in a chair because I'm pretty sure I just beat it by a lot. I was right—I did not get the job." – Comedian John Hilder*

How to tell if they're digging you

Because you've read every word of this book so far and have completed every single exercise in here—even the ones you didn't feel like doing—and because you've written out answers to the tough questions you could be asked, the interview is likely to go very well. How will you know? Look for these signals:

- You notice you're no longer selling yourself to them; now they're selling *you* on how great it is to work there, their wonderful benefits package, and all the perks their employees enjoy.
- Their language shifts from "The person we hire will be responsible for…" to "You'd be responsible for…" Their use of the pronoun "you" is subtle, but very telling. I doubt they're even aware of it.
- They're nodding and laughing. You feel they're with you.
- They ask other people to come meet you. They wouldn't pull them away from their work if they have no intention of considering you further.
- They give you a tour of the place. No one would make that effort for someone they don't think is right.
- They ask for references and samples of your work.

- They ask about your availability for a second interview or when you'd be able to start.

Just because things seem to be going your way doesn't mean you have it in the bag. Don't get too comfortable. You can still blow it if you let your guard down. And keep in mind that it's not a done deal until you have an offer and actually start working. I've seen too many people assume the job was theirs, and so they put their search on hold while they waited for an offer. An offer that, for whatever reason, never came. That could mean weeks, or months, of wasted time.

To take it a step further, I'd worry if a company seems a little *too* keen on you and wants you on board ASAP. Reminds me of the guy in my single years who asked me to marry him on the first date. Be wary if you sense desperation. Whatever lurks behind it is not going to be pretty.

Using humor during the interview

Whether you're interviewing or simply being yourself in real life, humor is one of the best ways to seem personable and likeable. A sense of humor increases the likelihood of being remembered and is one of the top characteristics considered in the candidate comparison and selection process.

If you're naturally funny and integrate humor into the way you communicate, then feel free to use it. Be careful, though. Humor is subjective; the same line that makes someone die laughing might be offensive to the next person, and a lot of people these days are super sensitive. For many of us, the best humor involves sarcasm or complaining or crossing the line in any number of delightful ways—none of which are likely to be appreciated in a business setting.

To make your sense of humor work to your advantage, you have to be good at reading the interviewer. If the person seems like a super straight shooter, your brilliant witticisms will fall on deaf ears. On the other hand, if the interviewer cracks a joke, that gives you the green light to use humor a little, too. Sparingly. Too much can be distracting and annoying; you're not there to entertain. If you're coming across as the class clown, the interviewer might think you don't take your work seriously. Balance humor with no-nonsense examples that show you can get the job done. Don't let humor get in the way. Your primary focus should be on providing answers to the interviewers' questions. And please, don't try to be funny or throw out a shaky one-liner. That could be disastrous.

As the interview winds down

You know the meeting is nearing its end when the interviewer says, "So, do you have any questions?" Of course you've been asking questions all along, but rather than say, "No, I think we've covered everything," pull out the list of questions you've prepared. Look it over to make sure you haven't forgotten anything and then say, "We've covered everything on my list, but I do have a couple of final questions." Here are those final questions:

- **What else do you need to know about me that would help you make your decision?**

    This shows you're eager to give information and are sensitive to the challenges of the decision-making process.

- **Based on what you've learned about me, do you have any doubts about my ability to fill this role?**

    Even I have to admit this seems a little ballsy, but man, the self-confidence behind this question is indisputable. If you're comfortable, go for it, especially if the position requires an assertive nature.

- **What are the next steps in the selection process?" or "Where do we go from here?**

    This will give you a sense of the process and timeline they've established for filling the position. The average hiring process is around forty days, which can seem like an eternity, but every company is different. You may have to go through three more interviews, a couple of assessments, a background check and a drug screening. Or they may want you to start next Monday. Try to get a sense of what you might expect.

- **When should I expect to hear from you?**

    Maybe the person is leaving for vacation tomorrow and the position will lie in limbo for the next three weeks. If you don't find this out, you'll wonder why no one's been in touch and you'll start losing your mojo because you thought you did so well on the interview, but maybe you suck after all. So just ask.

Before you leave, thank people for their time, and unless it would be awkward, ask for business cards from everyone you've met. That way you've have their contact information for your thank you notes.

Interviewing – After

Update your contact spreadsheet

"The faintest ink is better than the sharpest memory" says a Chinese proverb, so immediately after the interview, write down what you talked about in as much detail as possible. I say immediately because with every passing minute, you're more likely to forget something. Scribble notes in the car if you have to. Those details will prove to be valuable when you write your thank you letters, when you're called back for a second interview, and when you get an offer.

Update the spreadsheet you've been keeping to track your activity. Also record how you think you did. What went well? What would you have done differently? How prepared were you going in? Were you nervous? What did you learn? You'll want to review this so you can perfect your strategy before your next interview.

Send a thank you email within 24 hours

I've had many clients who've wondered whether thank you emails are really necessary. Okay, they're not as vital as oxygen, and if your skill set is unique and in high demand, you'll probably get an offer no matter what. But if several candidates are competing for a position, the ones who send a thoughtful thank you are likely to receive extra credit points, giving them an edge over the lazybones who couldn't bother to spend a few minutes on simple business etiquette. Now, if the interviewer was super weird or rude and there's no way in hell you'd ever work there, you can skip it. Not everyone deserves your polite gesture.

Rather than regard the thank-you email as a chore, consider it as another opportunity to sell yourself. It gives you the chance to reinforce your interest in the position, convey enthusiasm about the aspects of the job you're particularly jazzed about, clarify anything you said that didn't come out quite right, or respond to a question that you blanked out on during the interview. As with all your correspondence, use a conversational tone that sounds like your voice. At the end, refer to the timeframe they gave you as to when you should expect to hear back from them.

Sample thank you letter

Hi, Matt--

    I want to thank you and your team for meeting with me yesterday and for being so generous with your time. I am confident I'd do well in this role, and I love the fact that we don't really know what it could lead to. I'm big on embracing the unknown!

    After I left, I wondered if I had made it clear that my current contract position will be ending within the next two weeks, and I will be available to take on a new challenge by the end of the month. Also, here is the link to the article I mentioned about the gaming preferences of the 18–30-year-old demographic.

    Again, it was great talking with you. I look forward to hearing from you when you return from your conference at the end of the month. Safe travels!

Sincerely,

If you never hear back

Believe me, I know from my own experience and from countless clients I've worked with that you can spend a tremendous amount of time and effort going through multiple interviews, putting together presentations, taking pre-employment assessments, and then… crickets. I had one client who underwent a series of interviews for an executive level position and they freakin' ghosted him. After numerous phones calls and follow-up emails, he finally sent a tersely worded email to his contact essentially saying, "Hey, WTF?" He was infuriated, and I don't blame him. Eventually, they contacted my client and showered him with excuses and apologies, but by that time, it was already game over. Why would anyone take a leadership role with a company that obviously doesn't have their shit together?

I wouldn't think of doing business with some companies due to that kind of arrogance or stupidity or laziness or whatever you want to call it. Smart companies realize the way they treat job candidates should be part of their public relations strategy. If you still haven't heard anything after you've followed up several times, send one last email. I know you want to say, "What the hell is wrong with you that you can't take two minutes to reply to an email?" but instead just ask for a quick status update and mentally tell them to kiss your ass.

What? I didn't get the job???

You thoroughly prepared for the interview and executed it with perfection. You articulated your value concisely, the words flowing from your mouth like literature. You were witty and charming and confident, and quite frankly, irresistible. It's no surprise that they send you an email saying how much they appreciate your interest in the position and how impressed they were with your background and industry knowledge, and... *what?* They've decided to proceed with another candidate??? The bastards!

Don't let rejection break your spirit. If you're not offered a job, you can choose to talk yourself into a downward spiral, convincing yourself that no one will ever hire you and that trying something new was a big mistake and you should just learn to live with the status quo. Or you can choose to find out why you weren't selected. That's what I did after receiving a rejection email for a training position with a major hospitality and gaming corporation. After the initial interview, the training director asked me to come back and present a forty-five-minute mock training session to her team. Although they provided the curriculum, it still took significant effort—meaning numerous hours of my time—for me to internalize the content well enough to deliver it with confidence.

I thought I pulled it off well. Everybody was smiling and seemed engaged throughout my presentation. So when I got the "thanks, but no thanks" email, I called the training director and said something like, "I'm sorry I wasn't selected for the position. Would you be so kind to give me some insight into the areas I could improve? Your feedback will really help me as I continue my search."

The woman said, "Of course!" and proceeded to tell me where she and her team thought my presentation came up short. She mentioned aspects of my delivery that never would have struck me as being significant and the team dinged me for not presenting content that wasn't in the training materials. I felt they were way too picky, and I got off the phone thinking, *Are you kidding me?* I didn't feel disappointed or rejected; I felt thankful I didn't get the job. In my mind, that team would have been a pain in the ass to work with. So... *NEXT!* My point is, instead of letting my rich imagination mess with my self-esteem, I made a simple phone call and felt as if I'd dodged a bullet.

"No" does not necessarily mean you're at a dead end. Their preferred candidate may decline their offer, another opportunity could surface in the department, the person they hire may not work out. If you're super hot for a company, graciously keep the line of communication open.

Sample post-rejection follow-up letter

Hi, Scott--

   Thanks for the quick response. I'm sorry I'm not quite a match for what you're looking for, and I'm crossing my fingers that there will be a place for me somewhere with ABC Industries in the future. Everyone I encountered—from the random people in the elevator to the team members I met during the interview—seemed truly happy to be at work, and that means a lot.

   If anything changes with the position's requirements, please keep me in mind.

Thanks again,

As I mentioned back in Chapter 9, rejection is an inevitable part of life. When you're attached to any outcome that *has* to happen, you're setting yourself up for disappointment. If you don't get that job, trust that the universe unfolds in divine order and a better opportunity is out there for you. How many times have you thought something was the end of the world only to find that as things turned out, you're way better off? If it makes you feel better, feel sorry that they lack the insight to see how amazing you are.

12. Negotiate the Offer

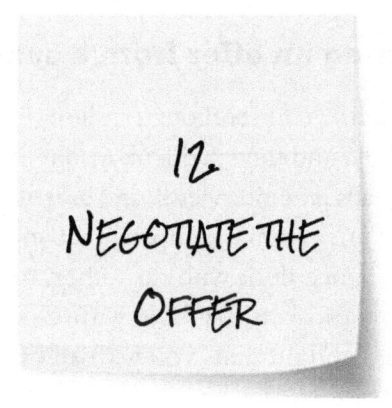

YOU FINALLY GET THE CALL or email you've been waiting for—they'd like to make you an offer of employment. Woo-hoo! You may be tempted to respond with, "Yes, yes, a thousand times *YES!*" but oh, no, you're not going to accept on the spot. Why? Because it's much more difficult to negotiate an offer after you've accepted it, and you don't want to start a new position regretting that you didn't take the time to scrutinize the opportunity beforehand. You need to look at it with a critical eye to make sure it's something you really want. You need to see the offer in writing so you can review the full compensation package.

So what you're going to say is:

"That's fantastic! I'm thrilled to be selected for this position. After I get the offer in writing, I'd like to take some time to carefully consider it and make sure we address any final questions. When would be a good time to talk again?"

Do Want You Want

It's perfectly okay to ask for time to contemplate their offer. Employers don't expect you to accept on the spot, and most likely they'll appreciate your measured approach to making such a major life decision. By phrasing it like this, you're letting them determine the timeframe. And during that time, you have some work to do.

But I might be getting an offer from a sexier company

When it rains, it pours, right? You send out a million resumes that are apparently accumulating in a black hole and then suddenly you're the most popular person at the party. You're getting calls and interviews, and as it always seems to happen, the "the bird in hand" offer comes from a company that you like well enough, but you *really* want to spin on the dance floor with this other, more sexy, company you've been flirting with. So how can you buy time with Good Company A until Sexy Company B gets off its ass and presents you with an offer?

Let's look at the facts.

You have an actual offer from Good Company A. The offer from Sexy Company B is still in the fantasy stage. If you feel your meetings with Sexy Company B have gone well and in real life you expect an offer to be forthcoming, there's nothing wrong with calling or emailing them and telling them the truth.

> *"I've enjoyed meeting with you and your team, and I'm very excited about the Sales Engineer role. I just received an offer from another company, but before I move forward with them, I thought I'd check in to see if you're close to making a decision. I'd love to be able to see the process through with you, and I appreciate any insight you can offer on the status of this position."*

Don't worry about seeming pushy. You're giving them the opportunity to compete for your talents before you're off the market. Fair enough. Here's what could happen:

- They tell you they're considering other candidates with strengths that are better aligned with their needs. Fantasy squashed, thank you and goodnight.

- Their response is noncommittal, and if you read between the lines, you might come to realize you're not as strong a candidate as you thought. Sadly, they're just not that into you.
- They reinforce their interest in you as a candidate, but they're unsure of a timeframe for making a hiring decision or they can't commit to having a decision before your deadline with Good Company A. If only there were a polite way to tell someone to shit or get off the pot.
- They confirm you're a top candidate and they'll see what they can do to expedite the process. If they really want you, they'll find a way to make things happen.

That last possibility is the only one that holds promise. But unless they've given you a solid idea of what their offer will look like, it could still prove to be disappointing or flat-out unacceptable. Therefore, given *any* of those scenarios, proceed with evaluating the offer from Good Company A.

Is it okay to ask Good Company A for more time? You could, but there's a tiny risk that they could take the offer off the table. So be gentle.

"I'm thrilled to be selected for this position and will give your offer careful consideration. In the interest of full disclosure, I'm in the late stages of the selection process with another company and I'd like to see that through. I assure you I won't leave you hanging. By when will you need a decision?"

This is a phone conversation, not an email, and ideally you'd communicate this as your first response to their offer. That means you'd have had to anticipate this scenario beforehand. If Good Company A is as good as you think it is, they'll understand and will appreciate your honesty. And having them know another company is interested in you could work to your benefit during salary discussions. Don't play games with them, though, or even think of playing this card unless it's the god's honest truth.

Evaluate the position

Before you received the good word, you probably mulled the position over and over in your mind. It's time to take it from your head to the page.

Just as you did with your current and previous jobs, write down everything you like and don't like about this opportunity based on what you know so far. Consider the responsibilities and scope of the position, the commute, the dress code, how you think you'll fit into their organizational culture, the company's values, their vision of the future, and anything else you can think of.

Above all, how do you feel about the person you'd be reporting to? Based on what you've seen, do you like and respect the person enough to want to make them look good? Keep in mind you weren't the only one on your best behavior during the interviewing process. What does your gut feeling tell you?

This is why you asked all those questions and looked for non-verbal signals during the interview. The more data you were able to collect, the better you can determine whether the position is right for you.

Likes	Dislikes

Take a look at what you've come up with. If the Likes far outweigh the Dislikes, chances are you'll thrive in the position and will find joy in working there. Nothing in the Dislike column should be a deal breaker. If so, there's no point in taking this any further.

Hmm... doesn't look good. After having scrutinized the position through the lens of reality, if you decide it's not for you, politely decline the offer.

"Thank you for all the time you and your team extended to me during the selection process for the Customer Service Manager position. After careful consideration, I have decided to pass on this opportunity. I would like to express my gratitude for the offer and hope you find a candidate who would be the best fit for your needs."

NEXT!!!

Evaluate the offer

If you've concluded the position should work out, look at what they're offering. The salary will probably grab your attention first and you'll have an immediate yay-or-nay reaction. Salary alone doesn't make or break an opportunity, but let's start there.

Salary

Based on the skills required and the scope of responsibility, does the salary seem fair? If so, great. Add that to your Likes column.

If it seems low, consider the number of hours per week the salary is based on. Many government entities and non-profit organizations base their salaries on a thirty-seven or even a thirty-five-hour work week. If you're used to working forty hours per week, be sure to adjust for the difference. Exempt employees are often expected to work longer hours. What do you expect a typical work week to look like? Maybe it doesn't matter to you, but I'd want to know what they think my time is worth given the number of hours they plan on taking from my personal life.

Chapter 12. Negotiate the Offer

Vacation, sick days, personal time, and holidays

Sadly, the average American worker enjoys only two weeks of annual vacation time, and some companies have the nerve to extend that benefit only after a year of service. I think that will, and certainly should, change as more employers get the message that people have lives outside of work and nobody can cram a year's worth of fun and relaxation into one measly fortnight.

Some organizations combine vacation, sick, and personal time and call it paid time off, or PTO. Fifteen days of total PTO is pretty standard for entry- to mid-career level positions, three weeks of vacation or twenty days of PTO for new employees is decent, and anything more is unusual. I like to think the more generous a company's vacation policy, the more they appreciate not only the well-being of their employees, but the productivity associated with higher morale and lower burnout. They might also be making up for what they're able to offer in salary, as often is the case with non-profits that have tight fiscal constraints.

Paid holidays are generally offered in addition to the PTO that encompasses vacation, sick and personal time, but some companies include holiday time in PTO. Most private companies recognize just the six major holidays; others observe all the federal holidays. If the organization runs 24/7, find out what their policy is if you work on a holiday. Would you get overtime? Comp time that you could use in the future? Or would taking a holiday come out of your PTO?

The bottom line is to find out exactly what they're offering you in terms of holidays and PTO, and how that time accrues.

Insurance and health benefits

If insurance is huge to you, ask to see a summary of the company's health plan options. Consider these questions:

- Of the plans they offer, will one meet your needs?
- How long is the waiting period?
- Would you be covered for a pre-existing condition? Are there any other restrictions?
- How much would you have to pay toward the cost of the premium? How does that compare to what you currently pay?
- Do they offer dental, vision, long-term care, and life insurance?

- Do they offer short-term and long-term disability coverage?
- Do they offer a health savings account (HSA) benefit?

Retirement benefits

Have at least a basic understanding of the company's retirement benefits, which could encompass various types of investment options, employee stock ownership plans, and profit-sharing plans. Ask to see their offerings and eligibility requirements. For 401(k) programs, find out what their employer match is. You may want to inquire about their vesting schedule. Do they offer immediate vesting, meaning you keep all of the employer's contributions if you leave the company at any time? Otherwise, how long would you have to stay with the company in order to keep their contributions?

Other perks

What do they offer to sweeten the pot? Perks may include bonuses; an employee discount; gym membership; a company vehicle; memberships in professional organizations; and reimbursement for tuition, licenses, and certifications or other types of professional development.

෩෬

You don't need to have an in-depth understanding of the entire compensation package before you accept an offer, only the parts that mean the most to you. If you're perfectly happy getting insurance through your partner's employer, then there's no need to grill the company on their health plans. On the other hand, if going back to school is a twinkle in your eye, you'll want to know the details of their tuition reimbursement policy.

Make a list of what you still need to know. If you've talked with someone in HR during the interview process, call or email that person and ask the questions that fall under their realm. That way you'll be better prepared when you negotiate with the person who extended the offer.

Once you've collected as much information as you can about the compensation package, add items to your Likes and Dislikes as applicable. Then ask yourself,

- Where does this opportunity lie on an awesomeness scale of one to ten?

- Where does it come up short?

If everything looks good, then by all means accept the offer without delay. Don't feel you *have* to negotiate and certainly don't negotiate just for the sake of it. If you're jonesing to do some wheeling and dealing, head to a garage sale.

Prepare a win-win strategy

If aspects of the offer are not quite where you'd like them to be, prepare a strategy to 1) address the shortfalls, 2) anticipate possible obstacles, and 3) present alternative solutions. That last one is important—you can't go into a negotiating meeting, tell them where they're coming up short, and then expect *them* to come up with a solution that you'll agree to. That's up to you to do beforehand. Also consider:

- Where are you willing to compromise?
- What's non-negotiable to the point where you'd decline the offer if you don't get it?
- How would you feel if you walked away?

You absolutely need to conclude that what they're offering you is fair; otherwise, you'll start a new position with underlying resentment. You won't have the motivation to make your best effort, and your first lousy day on the job, you'll be barking, "They're not paying me enough to put up with this crap!" That is not the way to go into it.

But it's not all about what *you* want; strive for a solution that satisfies both parties. Don't take an adversarial approach to negotiating. Remember, YOU'RE ON THE SAME SIDE. By extending an offer to you, they've indicated they want you to work with them. They *want* you to take this job. And you wouldn't have gone through the process this far if you didn't want the same. So instead of thinking, "How can I convince them to give me what I want?" change your mindset to "How can we work this out together so everyone is happy?"

If the salary offered is too low

Remember, salary is too low only is if it's less than what the market is paying for the expertise and the scope of responsibility the position requires. What your last employer paid you and what you need to pay your bills are not relevant to your negotiating strategy.

Don't get too hung up on salary. Everything in the compensation package that is of value to you has a dollar sign in front of it. Beyond salary, look at what they're offering that could translate to money in your pocket.

- Would you be getting additional paid holidays or other time off that you don't currently enjoy?
- If their health benefits are generous, what kind of savings will you see in insurance premiums and medical bills?
- If you're planning to go back to school, how much would you save in tuition costs?
- If they offer the option to work remotely, how much might you save in gas, lunches, clothes, and contributions to coworkers' birthdays and other social obligations?

If you're still not feeling good about the salary, even after you've looked at the package from all angles, you might address the issue like this:

"I'm very excited by the prospect of working here, and I know I can immediately contribute in a valuable way. I appreciate the offer at $X, but based on my research of the local market, I was hoping you'd come in at the $Y range. Can we look at a salary of $Y for this position?"

You've addressed the shortfall, now anticipate the obstacle. They may respond with, "The salary we offered is what we have budgeted for the position, and we feel it's fair." This may sound like it's the end of the conversation, but it's not. Don't back down. Continue to show your enthusiasm and confidence in your ability to meet their needs. Be prepared to present an alternative.

"I understand, and I want to reiterate how excited I am at the prospect of working with you and your team. It seems that my skills are perfectly suited for this opportunity. Considering both the scope of responsibility for the position, along with the years of experience that I offer, I think the market would support a salary of $Y. Can we compromise with $Z?"

Don't say anything else. Don't try to fill in any silence with more words or justifications. Hopefully, they'll reply with something like, "You'll really be stretching us, but I'll see what we can do."

If they've made it clear that the salary offered is firm, give them an option to consider.

"Let's see how we can make this a win for both of us. I understand you can't offer a higher offer initially. Would you be open to reevaluating my salary once I've proven myself, say, in six months?"

Negotiating other benefits

If you know for sure that you won't be taking advantage of some of the benefits they offer, ask if they'd be willing to apply their cost to your salary. When I was offered my last job, everything in the package was fantastic except the pay. I didn't need to take advantage of their health insurance plan, so I asked if they'd be willing to apply their contribution to my salary. They did, and everybody was happy.

Today, I'm not as optimistic about that strategy. Many employers won't negotiate salary based on benefits a prospective employee says they'll decline. I can see why. You may be getting health insurance through your partner, but if your partner gets laid off, then you'd be eligible to begin coverage with your employer. Employers don't want to risk paying a higher salary in lieu of benefits only to have the person opt for the benefits after all.

What would get you psyched about taking this job? Would flexible hours make your life a thousand times easier? Would an extra week of vacation mean the world to you? Put that on the table for discussion.

☙❧

Be polite, appreciative, and diplomatic throughout the negotiating process. Don't ask for anything outlandish like a month of vacation beyond what they offered. In my younger and more stupid days, I once asked for five weeks of vacation. That shut them right down and they rescinded the offer. Yup, that can happen, so don't be crazy and don't split hairs. One of my executive clients pushed too hard for a couple of thousand dollars that at his level, shouldn't have been a deal breaker, and he lost the opportunity. If you become a pain in their ass, they'll be done with you.

Execute your strategy with confidence

Most negotiations are done in person or over the phone, though it's possible to negotiate through email. While email allows you to articulate your message more carefully, and email may seem less scary, it's not the best approach since you lose the nuances of tone and body language. If the prospective employer clearly prefers to communicate by email, then of course play by their rules, but make sure your tone is conversational and conveys your intentions.

If you're not comfortable negotiating, don't think you're alone. Most people dread it. My husband is one of those oddballs who gets a thrill out of it. Garage sales, estate sales, pawn shops… whether he's buying or selling, Mike is *on*. I've watched him haggle with a manager at Target like he's in a street market in Marrakech. The price tag on our couch was several hundred dollars higher than what Mike paid for it. I watched him approach the salesman on the furniture showroom. "Look, between us," he said in hush-hush voice, "I couldn't care less, but the wife really likes this couch. Here's five hundred bucks. Cash. My truck is already backed up to your door. Let me take this off your hands."

The guy took the five hundred-dollar bills, shook his head in wonder and replied, "You are good, sir. You are good."

Negotiating doesn't come naturally to me, but with Mike as my inspiration, I don't think twice about asking for a price match, and I have no problem saying, "Is that the best you can do?" Learn to take advantage of opportunities to practice being ballsy so when it comes to negotiating an offer, you'll have the confidence to step out of your comfort zone.

Women in particular are known to do better when negotiating on behalf of someone else. If it helps, think of how a higher salary or more vacation time would benefit your family. Force yourself if you have to; this is no time to be timid. You're not asking for anything you don't deserve.

If you're worried about seeming pushy, I guarantee you won't. Overly aggressive people have no clue they're coming across that way. The fact that you have that concern means you are *not* overly aggressive, and many employers look more favorably on candidates who negotiate. They see them as high performers who think enough of themselves to ask for what they're worth.

Nearly three-quarters of candidates who ask for a salary boost receive it. I can't stress enough how important it is to come in as high as you can. Your future earnings are based on the figure you start out with. When you compound the difference on an annual basis, the result is dramatic. A few minutes of discomfort could ultimately mean tens of thousands of dollars in your bank account.

Here's another fact: You won't be offered a higher salary or whatever else you want if you don't ask for it. I can say with one hundred percent certainty that if you don't ask, you'll get whatever they feel like giving.

෨෯

After you've verbally accepted the position, confirm that they'll be sending you an updated offer in writing. Ambiguity can cause things to get weird.

> *"A couple of days after I interviewed with a high-end retailer on the Las Vegas Strip, they asked me to attend their orientation. Someone from corporate introduced me as their new assistant manager. I worked two days helping them set up their new store, and two days later they gave me a schedule. They never actually offered me the job; I just went with the flow. I decided to stay with my old job and never went back. I still don't know what happened, but I think I worked there for two weeks without pay. They probably thought I was a no-show without realizing they never technically hired me."* -- Michelle T.

Make sure the offer includes the name of the position, start date, salary, vacation time, benefits information, reporting structure, and any other items you negotiated. You want to go into this new endeavor knowing exactly what you're in for. If everything looks good, get ready for your new adventure!

Start the new job right

You approached every step of the process that led you to this new position with authenticity. Don't stop now. By putting the "real" you out there, the people you work with can trust that you speak the truth and that your actions aren't rooted in some self-serving agenda. Just being yourself—your kind, loving, confident self—will help you tremendously as you assume your new role and establish new relationships.

Appreciate your coworkers

The people you work with can affect your job satisfaction in a huge way. They can be a great source of support, a touchpoint of sanity when things get crazy, and they often turn into lifelong friends. Be good to them. See beyond the role they play in the company and get to know your coworkers as fellow human beings. Boring old "Rob the Project Manager" might have a really fun side to him that you would love to get to know. Look for common interests or philosophies or things you both can't stand. Nothing brings people together like a shared disdain; the bond I enjoy with one of my one-legged comedian friends was founded on our mutual hatred of celery.

Granted, some people are a challenge. Be a nice human and try to understand what's behind their disagreeable persona. People who seem oh-so-pleased with themselves are probably masking wicked feelings of inadequacy. Someone who is withdrawn or grumpy may have more issues than *Sports Illustrated* (ba-dump-bump!). Yet despite your best efforts to see people in a positive light, you might still conclude they're a total dipshit. That's okay. As long as they're not undermining or sabotaging you on the job, it doesn't matter. You don't have to hold unconditional love in your heart for every single person you meet. You're not Jesus.

Give your internal customers, the people you work with, the same extraordinary service that you'd offer to customers outside your organization. Respond to their questions with an enthusiastic "Certainly!" and "Of course!" instead of a half-hearted "Yeah, okay." Enjoy the look on their face when you ask, "What can I do to make your life easier?" Chances are they've never heard those words before. Seek their feedback. Make it a habit to ask, "How do you think that went?" or "What can I do next time to make this process run more smoothly?" (Don't ask, "What could I have done differently?" That implies something you did was wrong, and you never want to position yourself in that light.)

Give people credit in front of others and don't be afraid to share the spotlight. This shows you're egoless—an essential ingredient for success—and positions you as someone who's credible and secure. Thank those who've come through for you and ask what you can do to help them in return.

Look for ways to go above and beyond, but not at your own expense. Years ago, I worked with a guy who had an uncanny ability to add to my To Do list and I let him. I finally realized, wait, I'm working nights and weekends on *his* stuff? People treat you exactly as you tell them to. You may feel proud of your reputation as the go-to person to get stuff done, but don't give anyone the message that it's okay to dump on you. Find the balance of being helpful without allowing people to take advantage of your accommodating nature.

Keep the boss in check as well. Learn to say, "I'm happy to take this on, but here's what I have on my plate right now and these are my deadlines. What would you like me to put on hold while I work on this new project?" Remember, the reward for good work is more work. Set your boundaries early on or you'll burn out in no time. And keep in mind that (most) people aren't psychic—they won't necessarily know how busy you are unless you tell them.

Respect people's time

If you've asked for time on somebody's calendar, go into that meeting prepared with an agenda and a list of questions. Accumulate your non-pressing issues so you're not bopping into someone's office every ten minutes with a "quick question." If you need something, be clear about what it is. Think things through beforehand so you can make the most of your time together.

In theory, if you show respect for other people's time, they'll respect yours. That doesn't always happen, so it's up to you to nip unnecessary chit-chat or too many interruptions in the bud. A quick, "How was your weekend?" exchange is fine, but don't let anyone settle in for social hour. Every minute they drone on is a minute you might have to work late.

Here's a little trick to subtly give someone the "enough is enough" message. If you're sitting at your desk, shift your body toward your computer screen. Although your eyes are looking at them, the direction your chest faces subconsciously indicates where your attention is focused. If they don't get that hint, place your fingers on the keyboard and occasionally glance at your screen as if it's calling to you. If they're still clueless at that point, tell them to STFU. Kidding, but that's a satisfying fantasy.

Speak up and offer solutions

If you see something going on that appears to be unrealistic or unfair, suppress the urge to say, "Well, that's stupid" even though that may be the most authentic thought you had all day. Go through the proper channels and bring the issue to the appropriate person's attention. Never dump on people and expect them to make everything right. Come up with possible solutions beforehand and present the ones you think are most favorable. Offer to take ownership and to see them through; that way, you can implement *your* solutions instead of having to go along with someone else's dumb ideas.

Don't be afraid to speak up. You may be saying what other people are thinking, and everyone will benefit from your initiative. Progressive companies *want* their employees to feel comfortable voicing their concerns. The person who points out glitches in the system could prevent minor issues from escalating into a major cluster, and your resourcefulness in effecting change could be well rewarded.

Document your accomplishments as they happen

Remember the Circumstance-Action-Benefit (CAB) approach you took to identify accomplishments when you were writing your kick-ass resume? Here, I'll remind you:

The CAB approach to writing accomplishments

Circumstance: Think of a circumstance at work that needed to be changed. Maybe a process was broken, money or time was being wasted, or a need wasn't being met. Something was off.

Action: What action did you take to correct the circumstance or meet that need? How did you improve a process? What solution did you implement (or suggest)?

Benefit: What benefit resulted from your action? Plug in figures whenever you can. How much time or money was saved? By how much did your solution increase efficiency or productivity?

Using this approach, keep a log of every time you save the company time or money, retain a client, improve a process, or do anything beyond what's expected.

If you get into the habit of documenting your accomplishments as they happen, you'll have all the ammunition you'll need for your next performance review or when it's time to ask for a raise. This log will also help immensely when you update your resume or when you need to remind yourself how amazing you are.

Uh-oh, that sexy company wants me now

Well, well, guess who resurfaced? Yup, it's Sexy Company B, the company that couldn't manage to get their act together before you signed on with Good Company A. Now they're dangling an offer in front of you, and after you methodically scrutinize their package, they're looking very, very sexy. And rich. Good Company A has been… good. No complaints, but your gut tells you that succumbing to the lure of Sexy Company B would actually be a smart move for you in the long run.

Dammit. You hate yourself for even entertaining the thought of jumping ship. You were brought up to value loyalty, and your new employer, who spent all that time and money onboarding you, will not be pleased to hear you're leaving. You're not the type who takes a match to a bridge and now you're about to blow it up with explosives. Ugh, the guilt!

I get that, and if we were talking about a date to the prom, I'd say you gotta dance with who brung you, swing with who swung you. But your happiness at work weighs heavily on the overall quality-of-life scale. Let me frame it this way: While you agonize over trying to do what's right, the corporate office could be planning staff reductions and guess who's not agonizing over sending you out the door? Don't think that can't happen. I had a client who uprooted his family for a position with a major hospitality conglomerate here in Las Vegas only to be a casualty of a mass layoff a mere four months later. I can't tell you what to do, but I say put yourself first and pray that Sexy Company B works out, even if you're an atheist.

Uh-oh, this might have been a mistake

You did everything right. You diligently worked through the self-discovery process and packaged yourself with perfection. You won them over and carefully considered their offer before deciding to take the plunge. You were a helpful, cooperative coworker who suppressed the urge to correct people's grammatical blunders even though it killed you.

You should be happy. But you're not. Like a date who chews with their mouth open, no matter how nice they are, you know in your heart this can never work out. Maybe the person you thought you'd love to work for was transferred to another division or left the company altogether and the new boss is an idiot. Or maybe you simply don't love the company or this line of work as much as you thought you would. You fear you've made a terrible mistake, and you wonder if you can ever trust your judgment again.

Don't be hard on yourself. If you're truly unhappy, cut your losses. Do yourself a favor and start planning your retreat. Play along in your current position and continue to do your best, but don't wear yourself out; you need your energy so you can focus on what's next. Maybe things will get better.

Don't worry that a prospective employer will look at you in a disparaging light. If you've been on the job only a couple of months, you don't have to put it on your resume. If the topic comes up in an interview, say,

"Despite my best efforts in assessing the position and researching the company, the opportunity turned out to be quite different from what I expected. Rather than continue down a path that wouldn't be the best one for me, I've decided to be proactive and explore other options."

I understand that putting yourself back on the job market is a drag, but when you've done something once, you can do it again. It may not be what you *want* to do, but nonetheless, you'll never again approach it with the same level of apprehension. You know how to rebuild, and that's empowering.

13. LIVE WHAT YOU'VE LEARNED

YEARS AGO, I WAS BOOKED to do a set at the property that was the former Las Vegas Hilton. I showed up earlier than usual and sat alone in the balcony and watched the last half hour of Rich Little's show. If you're a youngster and don't recognize the name, master impersonator and comedian Rich Little was a frequent guest on variety and talk shows when I was a kid. After his show and before ours, we had a brief exchange during which he relayed this little gem: "Did you know Abraham Lincoln was Jewish? He got shot in the temple." And with a wink, he said those four dreaded words everyone says to comics: "You can use that."

Of course, I laughed politely, but was overcome by the reality of the moment. *I'm standing here yukking it up with RICH LITTLE in LAS VEGAS before *I* get on stage to perform stand-up comedy.* That's a scenario I could not have imagined just a few years before.

I truly believe that you, too, can achieve things you never thought possible.

∞⌘

I hope I've given you some good information that will come in handy for the rest of your life. I also hope that by going through all this you'll never again feel stuck in a crappy job or freak if you hear whispers of a staff reduction. You have talents and options and the know-how to always have a source of income that allows you to work—and play—with passion.

Keep this book handy and refer back to it when you need a boost of confidence or some straight talk on staying out of debt. If I could drill one thing into your brain a little deeper, it would be this: **Never let yourself get in a place financially that requires you to be tied to a job that crushes your soul.** Financial stability equals freedom, and freedom equals joy. Stay observant about what brings you joy. Reread the chapter on joy periodically to remind yourself to make joy the centerpiece of your life.

I have a couple of other things to tell you. **Don't let your body go to shit.** Your body is the vehicle that gets you around this earth, and it has to last your entire life. You can let it decay into a dilapidated junker or you can take care of it and have a classic car. The choice is yours. If you face health challenges because somewhere along the way you've been dealt a bad hand, my heart goes out to you, and I honor you for the fortitude it takes to get through each day. But if you've been blessed with a perfectly functional body and you're letting it deteriorate for no good reason, you need to put together a plan. Today.

You're gonna have to get off your ass. Move in whatever works for you, whether it's walking, running, dancing, lifting weights, boxing, doing exercise videos, or practicing yoga. If you hate the gym, don't join a gym. If you hate to run, don't run. Find a form of exercise that brings you joy and do it with someone who brings you joy.

People say they love their children and would do anything for them. Do you love them enough to stay strong and healthy so you can continue to provide for them? Do you love them enough so you can do fun stuff together as you age? Don't you want to keep yourself up so your kids will always be proud of how you look? If you won't take care of your body for yourself, then do it for the people who love you.

Keeping your body in decent shape is a form of self-love, and I also want to reinforce the importance of loving the person you really are. Even at work. No, *especially* at work. For decades I tried like hell to play the corporate game, and though I could fake it well enough to get by, I knew I was a misfit. I felt there was something wrong with me until I realized I'm not a corporate type—I'm an artist. It took me years to come to that epiphany, and once I did, a huge burden had been lifted. I finally understood why I'd always felt like such an oddball. There's nothing wrong with being an oddball—by all means, celebrate what makes you different—but you'll be a lot happier if you're playing the right game on the right field with teammates who also believe the only way to live is to be comfortable in your own skin.

It is possible to make a living without sacrificing your authenticity.

Truth, joy, gratitude, love, humor, personal growth, self-knowledge, financial stability, service and generosity to others, excellence in what you do... find time to work on at least some of these every day.

I thank and honor you for taking the time to work through this book. And from the bottom of my heart, I wish you a happy life that surpasses your wildest dreams.

Acknowledgments

WRITING A BOOK IS HARDER than doing a *Buns of Steel* video three times in a row. I want to extend my heartfelt thanks to every single person who inspired me to keep writing even when I wanted to take a match to this friggin' thing.

I'm crazy lucky to have so many friends, colleagues, and family members who've been an ongoing source of support. Some of you have been kind enough to contribute your professional perspective, segments of your resumes, or stories from your lives. Thank you for that.

My deepest gratitude goes to my crack beta readers and editors Ketti Blackwell, Sharon Downes, Joyce Weaver Conboy, Diane Weikert, and Mike Molony. I know you all have given up many, many hours of your time to pore over my words when you could have been doing something much more fun. I so appreciate your expertise and dedication. Truly, I can't thank you enough.

I want to recognize some of the special people in my life, starting with my children, Christopher Blackwell and Courtney Blackwell. You guys gave me the most important and rewarding job I'll ever have. I am in awe of your many talents, and I know I've annoyed the hell out of you by constantly pressing you to share them with the world. Sorry, there will be no end to that—you make me burst with pride.

My precious grandchildren, Connor Burns and Hazel Rice, are both destined to make an amazing mark on this earth. Connor, I bow to your commitment to public service. Your level of maturity has always astounded me. Hazel, you are pure magic; wherever your path takes you, it is sure to be lined with fairy dust.

I can't imagine where I'd in life without my beautiful mother, the Queen Mum, the famous "DeeDee Idaho." Thank you for always being my champion. Your undying support means the world to me, along with your willingness to be a big part of my comedy act. You can't help it that you're so damn funny.

And then there's Mike, my other gold mine of comedy material and the only husband I didn't meet in a bar. You are the most brilliant and insane person I've ever known in real life, and you crack me up every day. I adore you and appreciate every single thing you do for me.

Finally, I raise my glass to all the cool bosses and coworkers I've had over the years. No matter how absurd the environment, we laughed our heads off and made the most of those endless hours together. Thanks for making work fun, or at least tolerable.

I cherish every one of you.

About the Author

Linda Lou's quest to find a better way to work began with her first job at age fourteen, where she prepared dirty trousers for dry cleaning in hundred-degree heat. Since then, her career has spanned more than thirty years in training, technical communication, and career transition services.

A self-proclaimed corporate misfit, Linda understands the challenges of navigating the workplace minefield and the importance of finding work that doesn't crush the soul. She is all about living life with JOY and brings her *joie de vivre* to everything she does.

Linda's 2009 memoir, *Bastard Husband: A Love Story,* chronicles her adventures starting over in Sin City after a midlife divorce and how she got into performing stand-up comedy. In addition, she has had numerous personal essays published in anthologies including *Chicken Soup for the Soul: Divorce and Recovery* and *Chicken Soup for the Soul: Best Mom Ever!*

She welcomes personal consultations and opportunities to give humorous workshops and speeches. Contact Linda at lindalou@agingnymphsmedia.com.

Made in United States
North Haven, CT
22 January 2022